SEVEN HEAVENS

Inspirational Stories to Elevate Your Soul

RABBI LEVI MEIER, Ph.D.

SEVEN HEAVENS
Published by Pitspopany Press
Text Copyright © 2002 by Levi Meier
Cover and Book Design: Benjie Herskowitz

ISBN: 1-930143-47-8

Email: pitspop@netvision.net.il
Web Site: www.pitspopany.com

Printed in Israel

Dedication

In Loving Memory of

Frieda Meier
(1911-2001)

A Devoted Wife, Mother and Grandmother
Who Continues to Inspire and Bless

ACKNOWLEDGMENTS

This book was written during the last years of my mother's life and is dedicated in her memory. This dedication is only a small token of the blessing she and my father were to our entire family, friends and community. I want to express my deep gratitude to my dear brother, Menahem, for his continuous spiritual guidance. I value beyond words the many discussions I have had with patients, families, doctors and nurses, whose identities I have been careful to protect. All of the people and their stories related in this book are composites. Any similarity to any person is purely coincidental.

I want to recognize my friends who read the manuscript and made valuable suggestions: Lone Jensen, Arthur J. Magida, Uriela Obst and Fred Rosner.

I want to especially thank Paula Van Gelder for her exceptional, creative editorial assistance.

I want to acknowledge two brothers, Dr. Erwin Altman and Dr. Manfred Altman, who became my spiritual mentors and lived their lives based on their life motto of *"And Be a Blessing."*

TABLE OF CONTENTS

continued on next page

INTRODUCTION

IT IS NEAR the end of autumn. Storm clouds appear to be gathering on the horizon, yet I can still see the sun's rays reflected in the Pacific Ocean in the distance. I am sitting in my office at 10:00 a.m. on a Sunday morning, looking out my window to the west, when I receive an urgent page from the hospital operator. The patient in room 5947 wants to see you as soon as possible. He sounds very troubled.

I go up to the floor and knock gently on the door. A man's voice says, "Come in," and I enter. The room is quite dark, since the curtains are closed. It takes a moment for my eyes to adapt to the darkness and make out the figure of a man lying in the bed. His features are indistinct, but I can see two eyes looking at me from a head sunk deep into a pillow.

I approach the bed and sit in a nearby chair. For a minute or two he says nothing. I hear him sigh. He starts to speak but hesitates several times. Then the words come tumbling out quickly, with few pauses between sentences.

"I don't really know where to begin, but I need to talk to you. I am dying, Rabbi. I don't know exactly when. It might be weeks, it might be months, maybe even longer, but I know for sure I am dying. And there is nothing I can do about it. I've got cancer, stage 4.

9

Over the past six months, I've been in the hospital more times than I can count. The doctors just keep telling me the disease can be managed to some extent, but not cured. I've even seen the pathology slides. I've seen how the cancer has penetrated the cells. It's a frightening sight. It's so frightening that I am at a loss for words to describe how I feel about all this."

I remain quiet for a minute before asking him: "Would you like to try to tell me what you're feeling right now? Do you think you could put that into words?"

He pauses. "I'll try," he says. He is silent for several minutes. The expressions on his face change as he processes different thoughts. Then he begins to speak: "All of my life, all of my struggles, what am I now but a mass of decrepit flesh and bones? I feel angry. But it's more than anger. I'm afraid, too."

"What are you most afraid of?"

He thinks for a minute before responding: "I think it's not being in control of anything – my body, my future or my fate. Especially now, when my very survival is at stake."

"What else do you feel?" I ask.

"I feel very alone and depressed. I'm too afraid to sleep. What happens if I don't wake up again? What's it all about, anyway?" He is silent for a moment before he continues: "How can you help me? How can anyone help me? I want to pray, but I don't even know how to do that. Do you understand what I'm saying?"

I do not reply immediately. He has said a lot and I have been listening attentively. When I finally respond, I try to choose my words carefully. "What you are saying is very important," I tell him. "There are no quick or easy answers to your questions, but I want to explore them with you. First of all, I want you to know I will accompany you on your journey, if that's what you desire. I will make sure you are not alone with your questions. We'll meet every day to try to find some understanding and some comfort as we speak together. We will get to know each other better. First of all, how would you like me to address you? By your first or last name?"

"Jonathan is fine," he replies.

I take his hand in mine and continue, "That is a beautiful name. Well, Jonathan, I'll come back later today and we will talk again. I notice you seem very tired right now. Perhaps you will be able to rest a bit. May I open your curtains just a little, so you can be reminded of the larger world?"

He nods his agreement. "I don't think it will make any difference, but you might as well go ahead. There's nothing outside to see anyway, nothing but a bunch of trees with dead leaves. No matter how bright the room is, I feel dark inside. But you might as well open the curtains anyhow." I go over to the window, which is covered with two layers of drapes – sheer decorative ones and opaque panels made out of some heavy material that completely shuts out the light. I pull back the left panel of heavy fabric, leaving only the filmy white material to cover that side of the glass. I then turn back to Jonathan and say, "Before I go, I have an idea for you. Perhaps you will dream and be granted a vision of something that will help you along your journey, something that will bring you comfort."

"That's funny," he says. "I'm a scientist and I've never paid much attention to dreams. The nurse told me you're also a psychologist, so I know they're important to you. Do you dream?"

"Yes, I do. My dream life is very important to me."

"Frankly, I've always thought of dreams as neurons firing randomly."

"That's fine. Whatever you feel about dreams is okay. Maybe though, some image or sound will come to you and we can talk about it later. I would also like to remind you that whether you are

asleep or awake, you are never alone. God is with you."

"Do you really believe that?" he asks.

"Yes, I truly do. Now, try to get some rest and I will be back later."

At 5:00 p.m., I take the elevator back to the fifth floor and return to Jonathan's room. The room is still semi-dark, but some rays of the setting sun find their way through half of the window unobscured by heavy curtain. The outside light illuminates a picture hanging on the far wall.

"Good evening, Jonathan," I say. "I hope you got a little rest. How are you feeling? Did any images or thoughts come to you since we spoke?"

"I'm about the same, I guess. I did have some strange dreams, though. I think they came from staring at that painting so long. Have you seen that picture on the wall? The one with the ship on the ocean? Take a look at it. Maybe it will help you understand some of the images that have been haunting my dreams."

I approach the nautical scene hanging on the wall. Up close, I can make out some details. The picture captures a particular moment off the coast of some foreign shore. The perspective is from the ocean looking back at the land. Even though the sun is shining, the gray waters are rough and churning. One small boat, held in place by a thick rope, is docked at a small pier in the harbor. No one seems to be aboard. Another boat, the focal point of the picture, is in the foreground. It is an old sailboat with a high mast and it is heading out to sea.

"That's an interesting picture, Jonathan."

"I think so, too. I keep looking at the ships. The one in the harbor seems safe and snug. I'm worried about the one that's going out on the ocean. I even saw something like that in my dream, but it was different. In my dream, I looked and looked, trying to make out the face of the captain, but he never turned to me. The water in the

ocean was even darker than in the picture and it looked like a storm was approaching. I'm not sure if I was looking at the boat or if I was on it. Even though the boat was bobbing back and forth, I didn't feel too frightened. And somewhere inside the boat I saw light, something almost glowing with brightness. Then I heard a name. I don't know what to make of it. The name was Uriel. It sounds Biblical. What could that possibly mean?"

"These are fascinating images. We can continue to explore them. But I find it very interesting that the name Uriel came to you in your dream. It is Hebrew for 'My light is God,' and is the name of one of the angels who watches over us. As a matter of fact, it's customary to ask Uriel to go before us as one of our guides and protectors."

"This is almost funny. I have enough trouble with dreams. Now you're talking to me about angels. You remind me a little of my grandfather. I have to tell you that I've spent the last ten years working on the human genome project. I believe in DNA and I'm not sure what else. But what the hell, what have I got to lose at this point? Okay, let's say there's an Uriel. What could he possibly want with me now?"

"I think as we speak, you will discover the answer yourself. There may be more than one answer. For example, you have spoken about being very afraid. Do you think one message conveyed by the image of Uriel may be for you not to be so afraid of the unknown? His comforting image might lead us both to understand that death is not necessarily as fearful or terrible as you may imagine. Or perhaps, Uriel has come to shed light on our discussion. That reminds me, may I open your curtain just a little bit further to allow more light to enter your room?"

"Yes," he says. "And as long as we're talking about these far-out things, there's something else that I might as well ask you, although I can't believe I'm talking about this. There's a concept that has

13

been going through my mind recently, something that I heard a lot about during my childhood. My grandfather used to tell me people pass through seven heavens. Have you ever heard that idea?"

"Yes, I have," I reply. "But I'm interested in learning more about your grandfather and what he told you."

"I remember some things better than others. I spent a lot of time at my grandfather's apartment when I was little. He was a deeply religious person and I can still picture him sitting at his desk studying. He tried to interest me in things that mattered to him. He was very disappointed that our family didn't follow the traditions."

"What sort of things did he discuss with you?"

"Everything and anything. For him, being a decent person was the most important thing. He respected scholarly people, but his highest praise was for people who performed acts of loving-kindness. That was part of his message about the seven heavens."

"In what way?"

"I don't remember all of the details, but I know it had something to do with the journey of the soul. There were things you could do in the here-and-now that would influence your life on earth, as well as afterwards. There were stages that the soul would go through on its way to immortality. I must tell you that I don't know if I ever believed what my grandfather taught me, but I must have filed it away pretty well, because it still comes back to me after all these years. Like his talk about angels. Grandpa really believed in them. They had different names and different purposes. He felt that certain ones watched over him and members of his family at particular times."

"And how do you feel now about angels?"

He smiles again. "Well, you saw my initial reaction when you mentioned the word. What can I say? If you had asked me in the past, my answer would have been a clear, unequivocal dismissal of the entire notion as irrational. I'm still highly skeptical, but it's interesting how some things I have trouble with intellectually are beginning to appear in my dreams. Maybe it's part of the illness. I'd like to hear your opinion. You've told me a little about Uriel. What do you think about angels in general, the seven heavens and all of those other things that my Grandpa believed?"

"That's a fair question," I reply. "And a pretty complicated one. Let's explore these concepts together, shall we? Why don't we start at the beginning."

"I would like that very much," he replies. "Who knows? It might help me and I'm willing to try almost anything now."

"Fine, let's begin. But before we talk about seven heavens, we should talk about life on earth and what it really means to be human."

Part I

LIGHTING YOUR OWN CANDLE

PROLOGUE

Dear Jonathan and Dear Reader,

Life is difficult. More than anything, it is hard to accept that this life is going to end. For some, this knowledge is frightening, even immobilizing. What is the point of doing anything, accomplishing anything, creating anything, or caring about anything or anyone if our stay in this world is of such short duration?

I, too, wrestle with these great existential questions. I continue to struggle with them in the course of my life journey and I would like to share some of my inner dialogue with you.

I am reminded of mortality every day of my life. As a psychologist and hospital chaplain of a major medical center, I interact daily with dying patients. Every day, I recite the final prayers with those who are passing from this world. Every day, I hear their confessions. Every day, I cry with them. Every day, I am privileged to share these holy moments.

These people have taught me some of the secrets of life. Young, old, rich, poor, college educated and illiterate, men and women, alone or with families, the mentally ill and those who can function in society – each person who has died has shared something lasting with me during their dying moments.

I would like to share with you some of the insights I have gained from these people. I believe their words of wisdom and their experiences can guide each of us along our life's journey. They can also help us prepare for our final journey from this world to the world of the spirit.

"I hope you will share their words with me, Rabbi. I want to continue this conversation. But you must know, it's so hard to talk to anyone about these questions, these feelings, these fears. After all these years of marriage, I can't even talk to my wife about these things. Even at this stage of my life, I feel too inhibited and reserved with her. When it comes to feelings deep inside, my wife and I speak, but say very little. The truth we do share is reluctantly expressed. It's almost impossible to talk about our most private feelings. How can I put into words my fears about the end of life and the finality of death?"

Chapter 1

FINALITY

I HOPE I can help lessen your fear by showing you that death is not the end. It is just another stage of *life*, one which we can prepare for, just as we can for any other special occasion.

Most people cope with their mortality by thinking of death as something that comes suddenly and unexpectedly. Perhaps the most significant part of understanding death is that the process of dying starts at the very beginning of life.

Death accompanies life from the very moment of conception. No scientific discovery can change that basic fact. Life and death accompany each other until physical death occurs. Ultimately, viewing death as a lifelong companion, even a friend, endows life with meaning.

Naturally there is a delicate balance between being aware of our mortality – which is healthy – and being preoccupied with mortality, which can be immobilizing. If we can accept death as our natural companion, then when it appears, its presence will seem natural, just one more stage of a meaningful life.

Each of us experiences many types of birth and death throughout our lives. In addition to our physical birth, we participate in the birth of relationships, including marriage. We give birth to dreams, as well as to children. We give birth to ideas, some of which we act on and some of which just fade away. And finally, in the course of our physical death, we give birth to ourselves anew – to a spiritual, non-physical entity that is impossible to describe or comprehend.

Having assisted dying patients so often, I have become more comfortable with issues of life *and* death. I also realize more than ever how closely they are linked. One patient verbalized that truth in a way I found memorable. When I first visited Harvey, he told me about his gastrointestinal disease and its negative impact on his life. He went on to tell me that for fifty years, his wife Shirley was his source of strength. Since her death five years ago, he felt increasingly alone, adrift and unable to care for himself. At one point, he turned to me and said, "I'm not afraid of dying. I'm afraid of living."

I learn a great deal from the interactions I have with "ordinary" people such as Harvey. Of course, no person is ordinary. Every soul is unique and evolving. Those I am privileged to meet continue to enrich my life. I would like to share the stories of some of these special people whose lives have interacted with mine.

I have met people from all walks of life and have been blessed to find those qualities that bind them – and me – together. I have found the joys and the challenges of life have remained consistent throughout the generations. I would like to share some of what I have learned with you. And I hope my words will find their way into your heart.

"I don't know if words alone can help me. I come from a family that, although they loved words and adored literature, particularly Shakespeare, only reluctantly expressed themselves. They found solace in reading about other people's emotions, but not in expressing their own. The words in the books they read seemed to provide them with a safe haven for what they were feeling. But sadly, all the really important things never got said in our own house."

Chapter 2

WORDS UNSAID

JOHNATHAN'S WORDS express a condition that is not at all unusual. Most families maintain a conspiracy of silence. While family members live with one another for decades – eating, laughing, arguing and traveling together – there are many important things never said, as if by some secret mutual agreement. Those unsaid observations and truths usually involve the most sensitive and delicate areas of our lives.

Sometimes, as the life of a loved one nears its end, we are able to open up to that person and to other members of the family in a way we never could before. I often wonder exactly what it is that grants us the right to speak deep truths at such moments or to bring up issues from the past that have not been spoken about for years or even decades.

In other cases, such truths are never spoken. Sadly, even as death draws near, sometimes many significant things remain unsaid. When this happens it is only after someone – a mother, father, brother, sister, grandmother or other relative – is gone, does the rest of the family realize what conversations will never take place, what feelings will never be discussed.

What often happens in these cases is that family members feel the need for closure after their loved one's death. People handle this need in different ways. Occasionally, when I officiate at a funeral, someone will ask if they can put an item into the coffin with the deceased. It may be a photograph or a holy book. A number of times, a relative has asked to put a sealed letter into the casket.

I can certainly understand what motivates people to reach out in this way, to communicate on some level with the person who has left them. Quite frankly, though, a part of me has always wondered exactly what went into a message of this type. Recently, a 35-year-old woman, who had just lost her 72-year-old mother, allowed me to share some of her deepest secrets. She provided me with a copy of the letter she put in her mother's casket and allowed me to quote from it in a way that would disguise her identity.

> Dear Mom,
>
> This is the hardest thing I've ever had to write and I wish I didn't have to write it, but I feel such a need. I wish we would have talked about so many things and now there is no time.
>
> We've often said, "I love you" to each other, and for that I'm eternally grateful. I don't have to feel guilty about something so basic, which many of my friends have wrestled with. I have so many special, precious memories, like the red-and-white polka dot dress you sewed for me when I was in third grade. I remember how you were always so accurate when you put your hand on my forehead and said: "You've got a fever; it's about 100."
>
> And it was.
>
> I remember after I had my wisdom teeth removed, I was in such pain and so afraid. When I woke up in the middle of the night, kind of disoriented and scared by the bleeding, you welcomed me into your bed until morning. I felt a little foolish, needing you at a time like that – at that age – but

you told me not to be embarrassed, that everything was going to be okay.

There were many good times. I loved the Sunday picnics with our cousins' club. I liked your potato salad. It's still the best I ever had. I loved it when we would go down to the beach on summer evenings, after Dad came home from work. You made sandwiches out of leftover roast beef and it tasted so good, even though it was cold and sometimes sandy.

You taught me so many things. And you probably don't even realize it, but the things that have stayed with me the most are the little things that you probably forgot. Once, when I was about six, I was playing outside and I purposely stepped on some ants that were crawling from one crack to another in the driveway. You said: "Don't do that! This is where they live. It's different if they come into our house and get into our cupboards. But they live outside and they have every right to be here. You have no right to hurt them." I think I learned more about compassion and the feelings of others from that episode than from almost any other experience.

You spent a lot of time with me at the park. You pushed me on the swings and watched me on the teeter-totter. You laughed when I laughed, even though you sometimes seemed so worried that I would fall and hurt myself.

You always tried to reassure me about everything. But I have to tell you the truth. There were a lot of times when I was afraid and upset and I couldn't come to you. Sometimes, when you and Dad were fighting, it made me very nervous to hear your raised voices down the hall. Even though I couldn't hear the words, the tone really frightened me and I thought that the two of you would split up forever. Maybe sometimes I even wanted that.

It's taken me a long time to understand and accept that Dad was an alcoholic and that he was abusive. He used to really scare me sometimes. I remember when he ripped the phone out of the wall and threw it across the room. How do you think I felt when he smashed some of our good dishes? When he put his hands around your neck and almost choked you in front of us? I thought he was going to kill you. Can you possibly imagine my terror? But you never could leave him. I still don't understand why. Maybe you were too afraid that you couldn't make it on your own. Maybe you actually believed his apologies and his promises never to act that way again. But you pretended that a lot of things didn't happen. And you had the rest of us pretending, too. I spent a long time wondering if other families were like ours, if they had the same sorts of secrets.

You probably thought that David and I didn't notice everything that went on between you and Dad, but we did. We saw and heard everything. And we felt it, too. To this day, whenever I hear voices raised or people shouting at each other, I get a pain in my stomach. The terror I felt when I was five has never completely left me.

We talked so much about some parts of life, but not about how hard it is to live, especially with another person. I never trusted men and it took me years of therapy – that you disapproved of – for me to be able to see they are not all like Dad. There were so many things I wanted to ask you before I got married, but I knew you couldn't really answer them. I didn't want to follow in your footsteps and be a doormat, the way I sometimes felt you acted.

I know you always tried to spare us pain by ignoring things or not talking about them. But the truth is that your silence caused me even greater pain. You always talked about Grandma, but you never mentioned Grandpa. You never even showed me a picture of him or told me how he died. What happened? Was he in jail? In a mental hospital? Did he commit suicide?

How could I ask you about delicate things like sex when you never dared to speak of it or even mention it? You pretended it didn't exist. I've often wondered about you and what you were like before you got married. You told me that you partied a lot and sometimes drank too much. When you were experimenting with drugs, did you also experiment with sex? What attracted you and Dad to each other? It's so hard to believe and imagine you had a sexual relationship with Dad and maybe I shouldn't even fantasize about such things. But after all, that is how I came into the world.

I wish you would have told me more about yourself. What I know about you I only got from the glimpses you allowed me to see. Why did you often seem moody, even depressed? Did you ever seek help for those moods or were you too ashamed or too proud? From what I have learned over the years, I think you may have suffered from clinical depression and anxiety. You could have been helped so much if only you would have allowed yourself to be human and seek help.

I hope I can be a good mother. You certainly taught me about showing love, but I remember the things that made me feel bad, as if I could never live up to your expectations. How come you only praised me when I did well at something? How come you never gave me credit for even trying something new and challenging? I want my kids to be less afraid of everything, less afraid of the world and of failing.

I know no one is perfect. You were not a perfect mother and I was certainly not a perfect daughter. Maybe that's the way it's supposed to be. Maybe that's the way it is in every other family, too.

I needed to get all of this out. I needed to finally have one really deep talk with you, even though it's come so late. I hope you understand what I'm trying to say. I'm not sure that I've found the right words, but I know I'm speaking from my heart.

I wanted this letter to be perfect, but now I see that it is smudged. Those marks in the margin were made by my tears.

When all is said and done, Mom, all I can tell you is that I love you. I love you so much. I will always love you. And I will miss you.

I was deeply moved by the words of this loving daughter. Many of the thoughts she expressed are similar to those shared with me regularly in my counseling sessions. Many of these issues are universal.

Would you write such a note? If you start now to begin a real dialogue with those you love, such a letter may never have to be written. You may even be able to reach a more profound level of communication about those things that really matter. If we manage to say the important things to each other, we will be able to say goodbye without so much guilt or so many regrets. We will cry, but our tears will be cleansing, as they demonstrate our feelings for the loved ones who have left us.

"I do understand the need for more openness, more sharing, even of some secret thoughts and fears. But how can one talk about death? There's not even a vocabulary to describe it, let alone explain it."

Chapter 3

AN UNDERSTANDING OF LIFE AND DEATH

LIFE AND DEATH are both mysteries. The more we explore each of them, the easier it will be to pass through each stage of our existence. None of us knows *when* we will die, but we each know that the time will definitely come. How can we prepare for the unknown and unknowable? One suggestion was made by that wisest of men, King Solomon, who wrote that one's garments should always be white. This means that the way to prepare for inevitable death is to live a meaningful life – each day, each hour, each moment and with each breath.

Each breath reflects the special intimacy between God and His creations. In the beginning, God created the first person by means of a kiss, by *breathing* into him the breath of life. With that first kiss, the human being became a special creation, partially Divine. When the final moment comes, God will come and retrieve our final breath by means of a kiss.

So death is one of the most intimate events in a person's life. That may be why some people prefer to die alone, because they understand that this holy, intimate time is, in a sense, the experience of a wedding night with God.

During this holy embrace and retrieval of the original Divine kiss, each individual sees the Face of God and dies. And this earthly life transforms into an eternal, spiritual life.

During this special moment, few of us are able to let go and allow a loved one to pass into the arms of God. I have encountered a number of nurses who are particularly sensitive to this need to hold on. I will never forget a scene that I witnessed in the emergency room not long ago. An elderly man, frail and wracked with illness, had been brought in with heart failure. Near him stood his wife of 60 years. They had only each other and they were extremely devoted to one another. Mrs. Y. stood near her husband, crying softly. "I think he is gone," she said to no one in particular. "I think I have lost him."

Mr. Y. was being kept alive by means of a respirator and other mechanical devices. Soon the attending physician came over and said, "I'm sorry, Mrs. Y., but your husband has died. What you see on the monitors is the work of the machines, not your husband. There is truly nothing more we can do." After asking the doctor a few questions, Mrs. Y. agreed to have the respirator removed from her husband. As the breathing tube was being detached, Mrs. Y. continued to stroke his hand. He made a few involuntary movements and then lay completely still. He appeared to be at peace. The male nurse in attendance asked: "Would you like to hug him again and say goodbye?" Mrs. Y. went over and lovingly hugged him and touched his head before leaving the room.

It is natural and normal to want to express our love in this way. Such has always been the way of grieving. The Bible describes how Joseph behaved immediately after the death of his father, Jacob. Joseph fell on his father's face, wept and kissed him.

It is indeed very hard to let go. If we can understand that our loved one is now receiving a Divine embrace, it may be easier to give that final earthly kiss as we whisper, "Till we meet again."

"That is very beautiful, Rabbi. I like what you said. But I have to

ask you something very basic, something that I have a lot of trouble with. That is all well and good if we already believe. But what about those of us who aren't so sure, who have spent all of our lives searching, still struggling to believe?"

Chapter 4

TRYING TO BELIEVE

WHEN THE GREAT psychoanalyst Carl Gustav Jung was asked: "Do you believe in God?" he replied, "I know. I don't need to believe. I know." How can anyone reply with such certainty and conviction? How can anyone be so sure?

Perhaps the answer lies in the way we understand what faith really means. There is something beautiful about the origin of the Hebrew word for faith, *Emunah*. Most of us are familiar with a slightly different form of it – the response, Amen. Both of these words come from the root *a-m-n*, which is related to the concept of "nursemaid" or "nurturer." Hidden within that root is the word for "mother" (*em*).

When we seek faith, we are actually searching for an inner mother, someone or something to nurture us, particularly during the hard times.

Often before a young couple marries, one of them gets cold feet. Some actually cancel or postpone their weddings. Some just need reassurance from a dear friend or parent. "Get me my Mama," one bride-to-be cried out to those around her an hour before her wedding. "I need to talk to Mama now."

Similarly, at the end of life, many people seek the same sort of comfort. Dying patients, even when they are surrounded by other loved ones and friends, cry out one word more than any other: "Mama."

Regardless of your actual relationship with your mother, the word "Mama" symbolizes the person who gave birth to you and nurtured you. So as you reach your final moments, you may once again call out, "Mama," as you give birth to a new part of yourself.

Margaret is an 81-year-old woman who was a frequent patient at the hospital. I met her at the time of her first hip-replacement surgery. We had numerous opportunities to speak during her lengthy convalescence. Like many of her generation, she had left home at an early age. She moved to another state when she married and missed her mother greatly. Calling and visiting home proved difficult because of the expense involved. Margaret was devastated when her mother died five years after she had moved away. She felt cheated out of the chance for more mother-daughter moments and she grieved that she never had the chance to say goodbye. Several years later, Margaret was widowed at an early age and moved back to her hometown. But even in those familiar surroundings, she felt rootless and alone, with both her parents now gone.

When I entered her room, Margaret showed me a ragged brown teddy bear on her bed. "Please don't think I'm crazy, Rabbi, but I really need to have this with me. I bought it years ago, thinking it would be for our children, but we never had any. After my husband died, I realized it was really for me. I needed someone to hug. Most of all, I really needed to hug my mother. This teddy bear somehow symbolizes my mother to me."

Several years later, when Margaret was once again a patient at the hospital, this time in the cardiac care unit, she told me more. "Rabbi, I'm going to tell you a secret," she said. "You see my little bear here and you know that she's always been with me through thick and thin. Well, when I made what they call 'pre-need' arrangements, I told the people at the funeral home that I want her to be buried with me. I want to hug her at the end just the way I've hugged her most of my life."

I was very moved by Margaret's story and I will never forget her. She reminded me that we spend all of our lives on a mission of developing and shaping our comforting inner mother. And at the end of our earthly days, we may cry out, "Mama," seeking the comfort and strength we need to prepare for the journey ahead.

"My mother was a good woman, Rabbi, and I loved her. However, we certainly didn't have the kind of close relationship you describe in that story. To tell you the truth, she got on my nerves a lot. She always had to know every detail of my life, even when I grew up. I actually resented her constant intrusions. But she did get me through a pretty rough childhood. You know the frightening thing, though. When she got older, our roles were reversed. I was the one who took care of her. And it destroyed me to see how she was going downhill in front of my eyes. Near the end, she didn't even know who I was and I could barely recognize her. I wonder if my family will be there for me as I decline."

Chapter 5

THE SELF

WE *ALL* CHANGE throughout our lifetimes. That is a normal part of aging. Yet we are not always comfortable with our changing appearance or changes in the way that a loved one appears. While visiting a hospital room, I often hear a son or daughter of a patient say, "This is not my mother anymore." They mean that she is very sick and weak and she looks very different from the way she used to. She may not be able to communicate. She may be incapable of doing things she always loved to do, like baking cookies. We experience such losses as a kind of death.

However, each stage of growth represents not only a death, but also a birth. It is up to us to discover the new part that has been born when another part has died. For example, if a mother was very good at self-expression, but has now been silenced by a stroke, ordinary talking may be impossible. The challenge is to learn how to communicate in other ways, such as touching, showing photographs, listening to music, audio and videotapes, wearing special clothing, tasting favorite foods and displaying objects associated with pleasant memories.

I think it's important to correct the notion that "the person in this hospital bed is not my mother." An ongoing challenge for all of us is to view others, parents, friends or strangers, not just in terms of the way they look or behave. When we see a stooped, wrinkled woman walking towards us with a slow gait, it is good to remind ourselves that this person was once 10 and giggling with her friends, once 21, once a girlfriend, once a bride and once a new mother. When we gaze into the faces of those we encounter, we can try to search for all of the memories that are hidden there. And we can go even further than that. If we gaze long enough at the face of another, regardless of that person's age, sex, race, disability or economic status, we may also learn to see a part of ourselves.

"I hope you will be able to see parts of me that no one else can right now. I hope you will discover the young man who was strong, who served in the army, as well as the other 'me's' who live inside this shell. It's hard to grow older and lose some of your identities. Mama sometimes talked to me about when she was a young girl, although I admit I had trouble picturing her at that age. I know she loved me very much. Do you know what touched me more than anything? She once told me that I was a great blessing in her life."

"That's beautiful, Jonathan. What do you think it means to be a blessing?"

"Lots of things, I guess. Mostly about personal qualities and behavior. I think Mama was proud of the way I treated her. I did all the usual childhood things, but I always came through for my family. I would volunteer to help with the shopping or the laundry without being asked. I did more errands for my family than my friends did for theirs. I could always sense when my mother was feeling tired or overwhelmed. Whatever I did, I did out of love, and my mother's acknowledgment and her words of appreciation have always stayed with me."

"That's beautiful, Jonathan. I think both you and your mother were blessed."

"Thank you. I like the thought of being a blessing."

Chapter 6

THE POWER OF A BLESSING

NEVER UNDERESTIMATE the power of a blessing. When the challenges of life seem overwhelming, the heartfelt blessings and love from family and friends can help us meet whatever comes our way and go on with whatever it is we need to do.

During times of stress, even joyful stress, blessings become particularly important. At many wedding ceremonies, parents bless their children, wishing them well as they enter into a new stage of life, a new form of creation with a new partner. Right after reciting such a blessing, the parents often escort their child down the aisle, toward the beginning of that new life.

Something very similar happens at the end of life. Frequently, a dying parent will bless each of the children as they gather around the parent's bed. Now the order of the wedding is reversed. This time the children escort their mother or father to the ultimate marriage – with God.

I have been privileged to witness some very special moments of family blessings. In particular, I remember Louise, a woman in the final stages of her battle with liver cancer. She knew she was dying. She was conscious but extremely weak. She told her daughter, Natalie, that she wanted to see her entire family one last time. Her family had been very loving and attentive to her, but other than

Natalie, no one lived in the same town or had been able to visit her. One son lived in New York and another in Ohio. Two grandchildren were spending a year studying overseas.

Yet, when Louise's wish became known to them, every member of the family rushed to be at her side. Some came within a day, while for others the journey took a little longer. With each arrival, Louise seemed to perk up a bit. She had made up her mind and would try to wait until they all arrived. Her daughter kept saying, "Hold on, Mama." Just when it seemed as if Louise could not survive much longer, the grandchildren managed to get a flight home from Europe.

As soon as they arrived from the airport, the whole family gathered around Louise's bed. She immediately appeared more serene. It was hard for her to speak, but she managed, haltingly, to whisper these words: "I want to thank you, my dears. You are more precious to me than anything in the world and I just needed to tell you that. I want you to know how much I love you and how much you mean to me. You've made my life worthwhile. I am a very lucky woman. May you all have as rich and fulfilling a life as possible."

There was silence. No one moved for a few minutes. Then, one by one, each family member went to the head of the bed, bent over and hugged and kissed Louise. Each held her hands for a long while. The emotions being conveyed went far beyond mere words. Only the tears that flowed freely from every eye gave expression to the depth of emotion in that room.

Earlier in life, Louise had escorted her children to their earthly marriages. Now the children and grandchildren escorted Louise on her way to a Divine marriage. Each of these holy moments was preceded by a special blessing, given with total love. That blessing was one that will continue to be handed down from parent to child throughout the generations.

"That is a beautiful story and I can accept it when it's about someone else. But what about me? Okay, I've been blessed. I have two kids and some grandkids. But how can I, lying here at this moment, relate to the idea of a Divine marriage? How can I understand the idea of forever? What will become of me?"

Chapter 7

WHAT WILL REMAIN OF ME?

WHETHER OR NOT we have children, each of us wonders what our legacy will be and what will remain of us after we are gone. One way to approach that question is to search for ways to create something truly lasting. We have many options.

When God created the universe, He endowed it and each of us with tremendous energy and great potential for growth. We are free at every moment of our life to tap into those sparks of creation and utilize them to further the creation of the world. Some may create children. Others may create works of art or music. There is a universal desire to leave something behind of ourselves, something to mark the fact that we have been here, if only for a little while.

Great leaders have often erected monuments to themselves. In their minds, these statues and structures ensure their place in history. But such monuments do not provide an everlasting memorial. No one described that better than Percy Bysshe Shelley in *Ozymandias*:

> *I met a traveller from an antique land*
> *Who said: Two vast and trunkless legs of stone*
> *Stand in the desert. Near them, on the sand,*
> *Half sunk, a shatter'd visage lies, whose frown*
> *And wrinkled lip, and sneer of cold command*

Tell that its sculptor well those passions read
Which yet survive, stamp'd on these lifeless things,
The hand that mock'd them, and the heart that fed.
And on the pedestal these words appear:
"My name is Ozymandias, King of Kings:
Look on my works, ye mighty, and despair!"
Nothing beside remains: round the decay
Of that colossal wreck, boundless and bare,
The lone and level sands stretch far away.

Everything physical changes and decays. Even massive pieces of stone crumble. Can anything truly endure?

I believe we have the power to create something truly enduring. Each of us is a unique creation, with a unique ability to create. With every breath we take, we actually change the very atomic composition of ourselves and the world. Our words are also more significant than we may realize. Every encounter that we have with another person may have a lasting effect on both of us. Furthermore, our words create sound waves whose echoes can continue to be heard by others throughout our lives and even after.

It is not an exaggeration to regard each of our thoughts and deeds as creating enduring sparks in the universe, for everything we do can help bring more light into the world. In a way, our deeds become the flame of our own candle that emits energy throughout our lifetime. Even more significantly, the flame of that candle will shine forever. It continues to brighten the world. It will also serve as our everlasting memorial.

"That is a comforting image. Perhaps it explains what I was meant to learn today. I can't believe I'm saying this, but last night Uriel came to me again in a dream. He told me my candle was shining brightly. I didn't understand his words at the time. He said

something to me about passing through the first heaven and I couldn't imagine what that meant. But what you have just told me gives me an idea. Now I understand what my grandfather may have meant about each soul passing through seven heavens. Maybe the first heaven is actually here on earth, while we are still alive. It is our opportunity to light our own candles."

First Heaven

Lighting Your Own Candle
Life on Earth

Part II

GATHERING THE SPARKS

PROLOGUE

IT IS 10:30 A.M. on a Monday morning when I make my way to the far end of the fifth floor. I look forward to speaking with Jonathan again.

As I enter his room, I notice that he has allowed the nurse to pull back one side of the drape, just as I did. "I have a favor to ask, Jonathan," I begin. "May I push back the other side of the curtain and let a little more light into the room?"

"I suppose so, why not?" he replies. "Maybe you think the more light you let in, the more I'll see of Uriel or whoever it is I've been dreaming about. I don't know. Life is more complex than I thought. The more I think about my life, the more I realize that my own light and darkness have always come more from inside me than from the outside. I think I've always been lonely and depressed, even though I've never admitted that to anyone."

"Did you ever think of going for counseling?"

"No, I didn't think it could help. I must tell you that my wife tried to get me to go. Not once, many times. She said we should go together. But I never believed in it for me. I'm not sure I believed in it for anyone. That's funny! I keep telling you I'm a scientist and here I am talking to you about beliefs, values and feelings. Strangely enough, that's what all our conversations seem to end up being

about, one way or another."

"I find value in that. Do you?"

"Maybe. I'm beginning to think it's a possibility. Obviously I don't have all the answers and sometimes I can't even phrase the questions. Maybe that's why I need to talk things over with you. It's ironic, don't you think? My colleagues have just managed to map the entire human genome. They've deciphered the greatest treasure map in history, the key to the book of life, but I haven't even the faintest idea about the meaning of my personal life."

Jonathan pauses for a few moments. "I just feel so weird discussing any of this with anybody. Are you supposed to be the man with the answers who just listens to everyone else's confessions?"

I reach over, take his hand, smile and say, "I don't know if 'confessions' is the right word. I do know that I make mistakes. I certainly do not have all the answers and I'm sure I have many of the same issues. I think you're entitled to be human, too. I want to share something else with you. We all experience pain. And when we do, we all look for guidance."

"So you just listen to your own sermons and you feel better, huh?"

"Not at all. Sometimes my own thoughts and words fail to comfort me."

"But you're a Rabbi. I thought that meant being a wise teacher."

"That's not my definition at all, even though some Rabbis may be wise teachers."

"Okay, I'm curious. What's a Rabbi?"

"The way I understand the term, it means someone who struggles authentically with people and with God."

"Wow! I've never heard that before. Do you really mean that about struggling?"

"Yes, I do."

"So do your books give you the answers?"

"I don't usually turn to books at times like that. Printed words or intellectual discussions aren't enough. We all need someone who has internalized what the books teach and understands how we're feeling."

"So where do you go? Who guides the guide?"

"Would it surprise you to learn that I myself have been in analysis?"

"I suppose not. Isn't that part of your training?"

"I'm talking about something based on my own personal needs, a soul-searching I did long after I finished my official training."

"You seem to have a lot going for you personally and professionally. I saw one of the chaplaincy tapes with you and your kids, so I know you have a family. And you have a good position here. You get respect and recognition. Why would you go into analysis?"

"There are some things I do not ordinarily share with clients or patients. After all, this is your time and you are the focus of our discussion. However, I'd be glad to tell you more if you think it would be helpful to you. Would you like me to continue?"

"Yes, please do. I really want to know."

"For me, the catalyst for analysis was something that happened to a dear friend. We'd been close friends from our elementary school days. We even shared the same hobbies and occasionally went to a baseball or basketball game together. We got married around the same time and our kids are about the same age. Anyhow, when we were both in our thirties, he came into the hospital for some routine tests and was diagnosed with a malignant brain tumor. It was inoperable and very little could be done for him. From the moment that his doctors diagnosed him, they knew he would soon die. I didn't respond as a psychologist or a

rabbi or a chaplain, even though I tried my best to demonstrate my compassion and empathy. Mostly, I was just his good friend and I felt pretty helpless. More than that, I was forced to confront mortality – not just his, but mine. Things could have been very different. It could have been me. So you see, I had to deal with the very thing that we're talking about – our mortality, yours and mine."

"Thanks for telling me that. It helps me to know you've dealt with these issues yourself. Because you're also a psychologist, do you always have the right words to comfort people?"

"I don't always have the right words. I don't know anyone who does. But I will share something else with you. If I find the right words, you should know it's because I've been there myself."

Jonathan is silent for awhile. Then slowly he begins speaking, this time at a slower pace than usual. I see tears in his eyes. "There are other things, Rabbi. More than just dying. Things I need to talk to you or someone about. Stuff I've done..." His voice trails off. "I'm embarrassed to cry in front of you," he says. "No one ever sees me cry."

"That's okay," I tell him. "I cry too. I cry with other people and sometimes I shed tears when I am by myself. I cry for others' sorrows and also for my own."

"Aren't you afraid tears will be seen as weakness?"

"Not at all. I think being able to cry is a virtue. After all, it's the deepest expression of feeling. And even more than that. Tears are sometimes the only prayers that we have left."

Jonathan allows himself to cry for a few minutes. Even when he stops, his face indicates that he is still struggling inwardly with his emotions. After a while he continues.

"There are a lot of feelings inside, a lot of things I need to let out. I feel I can begin to trust you with them. Look, we've spoken a

number of times. I told you right at the beginning I'm no saint. And I wasn't always this old, sick man. I was actually pretty good looking. I may be a scientist, but I haven't spent all my time looking through microscopes, if you know what I mean. I was always attracted to a pretty face and I played around. When I finally did decide to settle down with Miriam, we moved in together and we were together for three years before we got married."

"What made you decide to get married?"

"Miriam wanted to. I would have continued living together but she wanted to get married. She never really said why. There are lots of things about her I still don't know. Wasn't it Freud who asked 'What do women really want?' I ask that question, too."

"Sometimes I'm not sure what women want, either."

Jonathan is quiet for several minutes. Then he begins to speak. "I'd like to confide in you. I've never shared this with anyone else. It's about our wedding night."

I remain silent.

"You know I don't know much about the Bible. But I keep thinking about one of the famous stories they taught us in Sunday school."

"Which one is that?"

"The story of Rachel and Leah. How Jacob was tricked into marrying the wrong sister. He only discovered the truth the morning after his wedding night. It turned out he spent it with Leah instead of his beloved Rachel."

"What makes you think of that story?"

"It's hard to describe in words. Look, after living with Miriam for three years, I thought I knew her – intimately. But on the night we were supposed to be closest, I felt farther apart from her than ever before. When we made love on our wedding night, I experienced something I never had before with her. She seemed to be holding

back and withdrawing into her own psychic shell. I saw tears in her eyes. I felt enormously alone."

"What did you make of that?"

"I don't know. I felt there was a change in Miriam after we got married. There was a shift in our relationship."

"In what way?"

"It's hard to describe. In a lot of little ways. For example, she used to be a dreamer and kind of adventurous. She was willing to take risks and try new things. But after we got married, she was more afraid of the unknown."

"Did you ever discuss that with her?"

"Yes. Miriam once said that it was natural for her to change. After all, she was now my wife and she could be the mother of our kids. She had always talked about wanting kids. She thought she'd find fulfillment in motherhood. And I think she did. Sometimes I felt she was paying more attention to the kids than to me. I actually felt isolated."

I am silent.

Jonathan continues, "I've been a pretty good husband and a good father to Tim and Laura. I admit I'm not that easy to get close to. I keep a lot inside. Even though I've told you about Miriam, she says some of the same things about me. She complains I keep a 'psychic distance' from everyone else. She says she sometimes thinks I have an invisible shell around me."

"Do you feel that way?"

"Maybe. I'm not sure. But I do know that over the last few years, I've changed. Instead of just tuning other people out and feeling numb inside, I've felt this anger gnawing at me. I sometimes blow up at all of them – Miriam and the kids, even my colleagues. I've got a short fuse and I can make other people feel stupid. I'm not sure why all that anger is there or why it's so intense at times. Sometimes

I'm afraid of what I might do. So you see, I'm not the person everyone thinks I am. I'm not just the scientist who goes off to do research each day. I've got feelings, I've got weaknesses. And sometimes I don't act very nicely.

"I guess I'm looking at myself more closely. I'm having some regrets and feeling guilty. Maybe it's just because I'm sick. But I admit I'm also a little afraid at this stage of my life. I really don't know where I'm going. And what about what comes after? How can I possibly imagine or think about an infinite period of time, something as unfathomable as forever?"

Chapter 8

FOREVER

FOREVER IS a concept beyond our limited grasp. Eternity is a word we use, yet never completely understand.

We normally think of eternity and eternal life as a state of continuous spirituality *after* death. However, a great teacher of mine, Dr. James Kirsch, showed me that eternity can be understood in a far more meaningful way.

Many years ago I was in Jungian analysis with Dr. Kirsch. During the course of my analysis, he became ill. He asked me to serve as his Rabbi during the final phase of his life. I felt honored and privileged to be his Rabbi until he died.

When he allowed me to enter his life, I learned about some realities of life in a new, deeper way. Most of our conversations will, of course, remain private, but there is one sacred moment that I can share.

Together, Dr. Kirsch and I recited a prayer that is often said before dying – *Shema Yisroel,* "Hear, O Israel, the Eternal, our God, the Eternal is One" (Deuteronomy 6:4). Dr. Kirsch told me that this Oneness is not experienced only after death, in eternity, but rather throughout life, in the here-and-now. Dr. Kirsch explained that although life and death appear to be diametrically opposed, they can also be viewed as separate parts of a larger whole. Death is part of life just as night is part of day. Similarly, eternity exists as a continuous presence throughout life, as a presence we come to recognize and befriend. Eternity can be found in each precious moment.

During the daytime we prepare for the night. We need shelter, food, heat and security from the elements of the world and from people who might take advantage of our vulnerability. Similarly, throughout our lives, we also need to create sacred space for the period after our death. Such *soul* work prepares us for eternal life. What we do with our soul at every moment of our lives can be precious not only for us, but also for the entire world.

We can think of that every time we perform an act of kindness, sensitivity or caring. We are actually changing the balance of the universe. We are adding to the positive energy of the world, which can be tapped into by countless others. We may never know how our deeds affect other people or the world as a whole. Our actions are far more powerful and long lasting than we can possibly imagine.

"I can believe that and it is a comforting notion. But I still have trouble with the idea of 'long lasting.' We live in an age when everyone, if they're lucky, has 15 minutes of fame. And here we are talking about all the time in the universe – something I personally can't understand. I don't know how much time I've got left, anyway. So what makes anything I do memorable or significant at all? How can I find some meaning right now?"

Chapter 9

THE PRESENT MOMENT

THIS MOMENT is far more significant than we may realize. In fact, all of life is nothing more than a continuous series of present moments.

When I entered the University of Southern California in 1975 to study gerontology and psychology, we were asked to collect numerous studies on aging for a time capsule that would be opened in the year 2000. In gerontology, as in almost every other field, a lot can change in one year, let alone 25 years.

Much has happened to me in the years since I left school. I have been actively engaged in a profession that allows me to counsel other people, to enter into the deepest recesses of their minds, psyches and souls, which is truly a privilege. One of the greatest truths I have learned from my own experiences and those of others is *we are each constantly in the process of creating an eternal time capsule*.

I understand this concept in the following way. Many people spend a lot of time planning for tomorrow and that is certainly necessary. However, being able to experience each moment is what actually allows us a glimpse into eternity. If we try to live life by focusing on the here-and-now as much as possible, we will store up the energy of each moment. Each of us can thus become a unique time capsule whose energy can be accessed by others and ultimately, we can change the world. Therefore, our essential goal is to experience the continuous present moment.

Laurence, a 76-year-old man who never married, discovered this truth in a rather unusual way. He has a distinguished appearance and demeanor. His full head of gray hair is always immaculately groomed. He wears horned-rimmed eyeglasses and presents a somewhat bookish appearance. Most people assume that Lawrence is a retired college professor. However, he is an entrepreneur who ran a successful clothing business for many years, one which he inherited from his loving but stern father. Laurence's work was almost the entire focus of his life until he retired at the age of seventy.

Laurence has always been good about tying up loose ends in his life. All of his financial and other records are kept impeccably. He has an accountant and a lawyer, both of whom he trusts, and he is in regular contact with them to make sure his affairs are proceeding smoothly. He has never been good at tolerating sloppiness or mistakes on the part of others. It is hard for him to forgive anyone's mistakes, even his own.

When he was relatively young, Laurence drafted a will. He wanted to ensure that his estate would be divided properly among his nieces and nephews and the charities he supported. Although many young people cannot even contemplate their deaths, Laurence showed characteristic level-headedness and good planning by purchasing a cemetery plot and headstone.

After his retirement, Laurence began thinking seriously about the headstone. What inscription would he choose for it? On a piece of drafting paper, he started designing his own grave marker, putting the year of his birth on the left side of the paper and a dash next to it. To the right of the dash was an empty space, a great unknown. All he could see was "1926 - ."

Laurence stared long and hard at the page. As he did, he was filled with an awareness that had eluded him before. He had always thought of life as a series of events, a series of years. There were the years he served in the U.S. Army, the year he graduated from college, the year he was named "Manufacturer of the Year" by the local business council and the year his father died. But now his attention was drawn to that short line in the middle of his sketch, that seemingly insignificant little dash.

At that moment, he realized that the dash represented all the years of his life, all of the precious seconds of his life. The date of his birth and the date of his death were not the most significant things after all. They would not be what anyone remembered or cared about. It was the *dash* that meant the most.

At first, Laurence was filled with great regret. He thought about all the things he had never done, including getting married and fathering children. But soon he found himself focusing less on his regrets and more on his dreams. Laurence realized he still had a lot of living to do.

He made a list of the places he had read about and decided to visit as many of them as possible. In the past five years, he has been to the Caribbean, South America, the Greek Islands and Alaska. He hopes to go to China next year.

His new attitude is about much more than self-fulfillment or doing as much as possible in the years he has left. Lawrence feels he never paid enough attention to social relationships, so he has been cultivating friendships and the company of others with similar interests. By attending a tai chi class at a local senior citizens center, he has made numerous acquaintances. He has also learned more about the larger world.

One day at the center, he saw a notice asking for volunteers to participate in a literacy project and signed up at once. Twice a week, he meets with an eighth-grade student who has problems with basic reading skills. Laurence sees himself as something of a mentor and a role model for this fatherless 13-year-old boy. He continues to derive satisfaction from knowing he is doing the best he can with the talents and opportunities he has been given.

Laurence has discovered something wonderful, even magical. If you live each moment fully, you are creating your own continuity, your own eternity. You are gathering sparks, transforming each moment into a precious time capsule that will be preserved forever.

Most anxiety about death is a consequence of not living fully in the here-and-now. The more you can live in the present, by doing for others and widening the potential for goodness and kindness, the more you can reduce your anxiety about death.

When death lies heavily on your heart, it is a symptom that you are not fully alive at this moment. You are not dying in the future. You are dying *now*.

So choose life. Engage in whatever you are doing to the best of your ability. Try to appreciate and relish each moment, whether you are shopping at the supermarket, eating a chocolate-chip cookie or playing with a child.

Even when you are ill and have limited mobility and strength, you can fully appreciate special moments. You may savor a conversation with another person, a melodious tune, a beautiful flower or the moving words of a poem.

Living in the moment can liberate you. It can enrich and add meaning to your life.

By appreciating and sanctifying each moment, you will come to recognize and experience eternity, even in the here-and-now.

"That sounds very uplifting and inspiring. But what about all the moments I've loused up? How about all those things I've done I'm not proud of? Sometimes I feel I'm a prisoner of my memories."

"Do you think memories are only associated with the past?" I ask.

"Of course. Isn't that the definition of memory?"

"Perhaps, if you understand it in a literal sense. But I believe there's more to it than that."

"What do you mean?"

"I look at life as a process of constantly creating new memories. You and I, as we are talking together, are reinterpreting the past right now."

He is silent for a moment. "That's interesting. I never thought of it quite like that. But I'm still left with the past stuff that I can't get rid of. I've got a lot of bad memories, things that bring me pain."

"When we talk about creating new memories, perhaps we can address the past as well. Maybe we can learn to see the past from a new perspective. That will also help us create new memories."

He is quiet once again. "I think I understand what you're saying and I like it. But what about the things I've never done and now won't have the chance to do, ever? I think I'm going to die of a broken heart. That's the way I've been feeling. I never expected to feel so bad about my past."

Chapter 10

REGRETS

EVERYONE HAS REGRETS. The question is not whether you have regrets, but whether you can still dream and hope. Death occurs when your regrets replace your dreams. Regrets imply a focus on the past, which only leads to stagnation of the present. Dreams open up new horizons for the future. Regrets bring despair.

Deathbed confessions include all types of regrets, including: "I regret cheating in business;" "I regret marrying him (or her);" "I regret cheating on my husband (wife);" "I regret not being nicer to my parents;" and sometimes even "I'm sorry I had children." Most of the deathbed confessions I have heard relate to three areas of life: sexuality, money and issues of emotional or physical abuse.

However, the most common regret, often expressed in the form of a confession, is not having fulfilled the opportunity or the potential of the gift of life. It is as if life were a burden and the weight of life unbearable. Patients often say something like, "I can't believe my life is almost over and I have never really lived it. I didn't do or say the things that are truly me, even though I may have fulfilled the expectations of others." Others may recognize that they were never able to appreciate the extraordinariness of ordinary life.

One 83-year-old woman told me, "I had a very comfortable childhood. We were better off than most of our friends and I had so many opportunities. My parents gave me music and dance lessons. I loved dancing and I even got an invitation to study ballet in New York with a master teacher. But my parents wouldn't hear of it. They were far too practical. They made me study education. So I got the degree and taught elementary school for forty years. But today, every time that I see a picture of a ballerina or watch a dance performance on television, tears come to my eyes. That was my dream and I never got to fulfill it. I will never have that chance again. Now I always tell my granddaughter to follow her own dreams."

Others have shared similar stories with me. One 67-year-old man told me he had always wanted to write but was coerced by his family into attending law school. He had a lucrative career as a corporate attorney and he enjoyed the trappings of wealth. "But," he told me, "I worshiped a false god. I was a slave to values that were not my own."

One patient actually said, "What a pity it is that I had to wait until now, until my body is riddled with cancer, to learn how to live."

A gentle reminder: Life is not a popularity contest. Life is not a rehearsal. Life is a process of constant growth and of facing new challenges. Try your hand at something you would like to pursue. You will discover that your anticipatory fears are much more frightening than the actual situations you will encounter. You may have to try again and again but the journey will be worthwhile. You may even succeed.

So dream, dream and dream. And when you have finished dreaming, dream again until your final breath.

"I feel like one of the patients you just mentioned. There's so little time and so much yet left for me to do. I'd like to make my remaining time count for something, maybe for my own spiritual growth if that's possible. But I have trouble relating to a lot of the things you talk about. You speak of God and angels. But I'm dying. What's so Godly, angelic or holy about that?"

Chapter 11

HOLINESSS

EVERY ASPECT of life – dreaming, eating, sleeping, walking or listening to a bird sing – is potentially holy. Yet certain creative and transforming moments are uniquely Divine. These include the birth of a baby, marriage, even the dying process and death itself.

I am very grateful to one of the attending physicians on our staff for allowing the residents he supervises to become more aware of the sanctity of each individual and each moment. "Never tell me about the 'hip' or the 'lung' or the 'intestine,'" says this wise doctor during the initial staff orientation. "Tell me about Mrs. Collins who is in extreme pain, whose husband seems to be at her bedside night and day and who is worried sick about her. This hospital is full of stories. You might have finished your rotation in one specialty or another, but you're certainly going to learn that no patient is 'typical.' No two illnesses are identical, even if the diagnoses are the same. They are as varied as the people who have them. No course of treatment is 'routine.' Each healing is specific to the individual. Think about this every time you enter a room. Each room is a new person, a new world. Respect the uniqueness of everyone in your care."

We must all keep in mind the holiness and divinity of every human being. When we enter the room of a dying person, we are entering a holy place, similar to the site of the burning bush, where Moses experienced a Divine vision. The bush was engulfed in flame, yet it was not consumed. Similarly, when a person dies, the body disintegrates but the soul lives eternally.

Moses was told to remove his shoes when he stood on holy ground and encountered the burning bush. When we enter the room of a dying person, we can recognize that this, too, is a holy place and moment. We should try to remove the veils around our hearts and souls, revealing layers of ourselves that usually remain hidden. In this way, we can unravel the mystery of who we are and what lies hidden beneath the expressions and personalities we wear each day. We will then allow the light within us to radiate and connect with the eternal light and soul of the one who is dying. We can help that person give birth to his or her eternal self.

"I like the relationship that you see between birth and death and birth again. The idea of an ongoing cycle is comforting. I'm in the mood to explore this theme further. Actually, in everything you say, you seem to stress wholeness, oneness and harmony. I wish I could share that view."

Chapter 12

ONENESS

ONENESS IS EVERYWHERE, though we often fail to see it. For example, we think of sunrise and sunset as complete opposites. Yet, of course, they are not. Let me tell you about a recent experience I had. During a brief vacation in Carmel-by-the-Sea, California, I went down to see the sunset on the beach. It was magnificent. Afterwards, when the sun was no longer visible in the sky, most of the people got up and left. However, I lingered for another half hour.

I thought about where the sun had gone. I realized that although the sun was no longer visible from where I stood, it would soon be rising over the beaches of China, half a world away.

This image of the sun can help us understand the cycle of the soul. As we watch the fading of a soul's earthly light, we can try to picture the rebirth of that soul in a new place, in a land we do not know. This helps us better appreciate the time of transition so we can respond accordingly.

Usually, when a person dies, family and friends are numb, shocked, tearful and tired. Then they frantically begin making plans for the funeral by calling a mortuary, making sure a physician signs the death certificate, and phoning family and friends to share the sad news.

But not everyone rushes to take care of these earthly concerns. I recall one person in particular, a highly spiritual woman named Barbara, who asked me to share a very special, holy time with her. She decided that she did not want to say a hurried goodbye to her father. She was determined to quietly reflect by his bedside for several hours after he died. She was sure this would help her father's soul begin its ascent and reunion with God.

Barbara let me stay with her for part of that time. She sat quietly by the side of the bed, holding her father's hand. From time to time, she recited passages from Psalms, poetry and other comforting words that had been meaningful to her father. At one point, she softly hummed a tune that sounded like a lullaby. These were holy moments I will never forget. As we sat together, Barbara and I felt privileged to be witnessing both a sunset and a new dawn.

I am often reminded of that link between birth and death. Connie's story is yet another illustration of that connection. Connie is a 37-year-old woman who had been admitted to the hospital to give birth to her third child. This pregnancy was very different from her previous ones. She seemed to be gaining too much weight too quickly. "It looks like I'm carrying seven babies," she told me.

Her obstetrician became particularly worried. In her sixth month, when Connie complained about pain, the doctor performed an ultrasound examination. What he saw perturbed him. There was a lot of fluid that didn't belong there. He immediately admitted Connie to the hospital for observation and subsequently, a Caesarean delivery.

She was wheeled into the operating room, where her obstetrician quickly made an incision and delivered a premature but healthy baby boy. At the same time, he explored her entire abdominal and pelvic area to determine what had caused such unusual bloating. He took tissue samples and sent them to the pathology department. The laboratory report came back quickly: ovarian cancer, stage 3.

Amazingly, with expert care and intensive chemotherapy, Connie made a complete recovery. When I saw her recently, she told me, "I gave birth to my baby and he gave birth to me." When I asked her to elaborate, she said, "He saved my life in two ways. If it hadn't been for him, I would never have been diagnosed in time. But even more than that, wanting to care for him gives me the will to fight and go on."

What could have been a story of life and death became instead a tale of life and life. As Connie's experience demonstrates, life and death are certainly not polar opposites. Each possesses within it the seed of the other.

"I appreciate your words and I feel that Uriel may have spoken to me again through you. I must be changing or I wouldn't even be talking to you in these terms. I really am trying to utilize everything I have been granted to treasure each moment. Perhaps I am passing through the second heaven my grandfather talked about, a heaven in which we gather the sparks of our own lives. I can accept that eternity exists all around us, in every moment, in every breath. I also see that we must try our best to recognize and appreciate each moment. We don't need artificial divisions between past, present and future. These are all part of eternity."

First Heaven

Lighting Your Own Candle

Life on Earth

Second Heaven

Gathering the Sparks

The Present is Part of Eternity

Part III

SHELTERING THE FLAME

PROLOGUE

IT IS AROUND noon on Tuesday. Jonathan was sleeping when I looked in on him earlier. He seems to require more rest than he did before. Now he is awake but seems weak. It is bright outside, and I notice that Jonathan has allowed the nurse to pull back the right curtain a little more. Now we can both see farther. In the distance, we see something shimmering. It must be the Pacific Ocean, way out there on the western horizon. The sun is being reflected in the water below.

"Can you see the ocean from where you are lying?" I ask Jonathan.

"I think so," he replies. "But I'm not sure. I've been here so long, looking at things from the same angle for so long. I'm not even certain what's real anymore, what really exists and what's simply a mirage. Someone told me that on a clear day, you can see Catalina Island, 26 miles away, but I've never been able to spot it. Maybe what I think is the ocean is just a shimmering layer of air pollution."

"That could be true," I answer. "But surely you recognize how limited our sight is under the best of circumstances. No matter where we look, we're limited by the line of the horizon. We can't see beyond it. It's the same way with time and life in general. How far can you see?"

"Sometimes, I like to think I get a glimpse of the future when I see my children and grandchildren. I like to picture them growing older, doing things and remembering me. Having children may be a way to make sure that there will be someone around to care for and remember us."

"Well, that may be one of the reasons. Was that true for you?"

"Maybe, I guess so, but I'm not sure. I have mixed feelings. To tell you the truth, I'm not sure I was really cut out for fatherhood. There have actually been times when I've wondered if it's all been worth it. I've told you a little bit about Tim and Laura. I guess they came out okay. What parent wouldn't be proud? Laura's a lawyer and Tim's successful in business. And they've even given me grand-children. But I've only been a little honest with you, Rabbi. I actually have another child, but we never talk about him. We haven't for the last 15 years."

"Do you want to tell me about him?"

"I guess there's no point in hiding anything now. His name's Jeremy and I don't know where we went wrong with him. I'm not even sure we're to blame – or I'm to blame. How could I be such a lousy father if I've got two good kids? Anyway, Jeremy has been getting into trouble since his teens. He was never good academically. I told him that was okay with me and it would be fine if he learned some kind of a trade to support himself. Well, that turned out to be the least of our troubles.

"The kid's never been anything but a source of aggravation to us. We even sent him away to a military school to try to get some discipline into him, but that backfired, too. He became even more rebellious. He started taking marijuana which led to harder stuff. The more money he needed to support his habit, the lower he sank. He's robbed, cheated, lied and conned. He's a master manipulator. The first time he ended up in jail, I bailed him out. Then I decided he

was on his own. We haven't spoken in years. I sometimes wish that he was never born. Sometimes, I feel I've been betrayed by life."

"What do you mean by that?"

"A lot of different things, I guess. So many things have happened that I could never have foreseen or anticipated. Like my wedding night, like Jeremy."

"Is there anything else in particular?"

"Not something I can really put into words. It's just the daily struggle of living and all the big questions of life. No matter what I've accomplished in science, the questions never go away. I wonder what I've really accomplished, especially with my family. I haven't been such a great father after all, have I?"

"I'm not so sure about that. I'm not so sure that anyone would necessarily judge you as harshly as you're judging yourself. Relationships between parents and children are never easy, at any age."

"Is it wrong for me to feel that I'm entitled to something in return for all I've invested in my kids? They're all I'll be leaving behind me."

Chapter 13

THE LEGACY TO CHILDREN

CHILDREN CAN CERTAINLY be a precious legacy. But so can parents. I learned that lesson from a very special mother, Martha, and her daughter, Sharon.

Martha and her husband were devoted parents and Sharon, their only child, brought them great joy and pride. Even though Sharon made friends easily in school and was active in various social groups, she always enjoyed a particularly close relationship with her mother. As Sharon blossomed into adulthood, she and her mother became friends in a new way – as two women, rather than solely as mother and daughter. At the age of 28, Sharon married and soon gave birth to a little boy. She had a solid marriage and felt fulfilled in every way.

Not long afterwards, Martha was diagnosed with a degenerative disease. She became bedridden and rapidly lost a great deal of weight. Oxygen always had to be on hand, in case her breathing became labored. Throughout the entire period of her mother's illness, Sharon remained steadfast, loyal and committed to helping Martha in every way.

Eventually, Martha was hospitalized for what she knew would be the last time. Her condition continued to worsen. She and Sharon had always been able to communicate well, even about sensitive issues. One day, near the end, Sharon sat at Martha's bedside and stroked her hair while talking to her. "Mom," she said, "you've always been great to me and a lot of who I am is because of you. I want to thank you again and tell you how much I love you. I also need to share something with you. I'm really going to miss you. Part of me is dying and will die when you die."

Both women began to sob and Martha said, "You've comforted me, sweetie. I'm glad to know you'll miss me, but new parts of you will grow and develop even after I'm gone."

In that room, a comforting transformation was taking place. Sharon gave beautiful expression to the truth that there is no one like a mother. No one else knows your entire history, from the time of the womb and beyond. No one else cares for you on that level. No one else nurses you at her breast. So, indeed, an irreplaceable part of Sharon would "die" with her mother, while new parts would also gradually appear. At the same time, however, a vital part of Martha would live on through her daughter. The circle of life would continue.

"I hope a part of me will continue through Tim and Laura. Maybe I should appreciate the two good kids I have. I do love them and I know they love me. It will be very hard to say goodbye to them."

"If you find it hard to speak to them directly, do you think you could express yourself in a letter to them? Would that make it any easier?"

"I'm not sure. Writing was never one of my strong points. I think I use the other hemisphere of my brain."

"I don't think anyone will grade you on style or punctuation. It's the feelings that count."

"But how can I possibly do that? Words can't possibly convey what I feel."

"Would you like me to share something with you? Down in my

office, I have several books by a wonderful Danish author, Jens Peter Jacobsen."

"I've heard that name before. My father discovered him later in life and thought very highly of him. Dad was always trying to get me to read more, but I never had the time or motivation. I didn't have much use for literature but I did appreciate that Shelley poem you shared with me. Do you read a lot of poetry?"

"Yes, I do. How about you?"

"In recent years I've gotten back into it a little more. For years, I read nothing but science. But my father always stressed the importance of the humanities."

"Please tell me about your father."

Jonathan laughs. "Have you got a year or so? Seriously, he was a brilliant, complex man who influenced me in more ways than he knew – or that I realized."

"What did he do for a living?"

"He was a professor of comparative literature at Stanford. He loved the written and spoken word. He enriched my life. You would have liked him."

"I'm sorry that I never had the opportunity to know him. But I am meeting some part of him now, the part that resides in you. And I am also getting to know the unique individual that you are. You bring your own light to the world."

"Thank you for telling me that," Jonathan says softly. He is momentarily overcome with emotion. He struggles with his feelings for a few minutes, not allowing his tears to flow. After composing himself, he says softly, "I'm sure I'm not the first to struggle with what comes after life."

"You're right. Everyone struggles with the unknown and there is a wealth of literary insight on this subject. One of Jens Peter Jacobsen's books contains a beautiful letter from a mother to her

children that I would like to share with you. May I bring it up and read it?"

"Okay, I guess."

I go down to my office and retrieve my copy of 'Mogens and Other Stories.' I bring it up to Jonathan's room, open it to page 149 and read the following passage [1]:

> The one who must die, dear children, is so bereft; I am so impoverished, because this entire lovely world, which for so many years has been my rich, blessed home, is to be taken from me; my chair will stand empty, the door will close on me, and I shall never set foot here again. This is why I look on all the world with the prayer in my eyes that it will care for me, this is why I come and implore you to love me with all the love you once gave me; don't forget, to be remembered is the only part of the human world that will be mine from now on. Simply to be remembered, nothing more.

After I finish reading, I do not speak. Neither does Jonathan. I hear some muffled sounds and I know he is weeping.

Finally, he says, "That's beautiful, I'll admit. The power of the words really got to me. But it's literature. It's from a made-up parent to fictional children."

"In one way it is fiction. But it is also very real, as you can tell from the deep emotions it evokes. Jens Peter Jacobsen wrote those words when he himself was chronically ill. This is also his own farewell letter. Even if you don't express yourself in these words, you are saying the same thing. Perhaps you might want to consider

---

[1] Translated from the Danish by Tiina Nunnaly. Seattle: Fjord Press, 1994; originally published in 1882.

sharing some passage from a novel or poem with your children to make it easier to say such things to them."

"I might be able to, somewhere down the road. I don't think I'm ready for that yet. I can't talk to my kids like that, at least not right now." Jonathan smiles and adds, "I guess I just have to hope that I can stay on good terms with my kids and that nothing really bad comes between us so they'll show up at my funeral! I can't believe I'm joking about this. But maybe I'm serious too. I don't know who might attend my funeral. I'm not even a member of any synagogue."

"Is there any special reason?"

"Yeah. For most of my life, I've been down on organized religion. I've met people who call themselves religious but are anything but that."

"Would you care to elaborate?"

"Sure. I've met people who say they follow the laws of the Five Books of Moses, but they don't act or sound any different from anyone else."

"That's a good point. Can you think of any specific examples?"

"Sure. There's a vivid memory I have. When my mother died, I wanted to honor her by keeping seven days of mourning, as she would have wanted. I remember that it's called sitting shiva."

"That's correct," I reply. "What was it like for you?"

"Well, all these people came, but it wasn't very comforting. I ended up comforting them more than they comforted me."

"What happened?"

"They didn't know how to act or what to say. Some of them tried to ignore the fact that my mother was dead. They talked about everything else. I didn't say anything. They probably thought they were being 'observant,' but I didn't find their visit spiritual or meaningful."

"Why do you think they acted the way they did?"

"I think they were uncomfortable with the whole idea of death. People can't stand to think or talk about death and dying, because it reminds them that they're mortal too."

"I think that is a very wise observation, Jonathan."

"Thank you. But I'm not sure I'm any better than they are. I also don't know what to say to people who are mourning. What's the real meaning of mourning? What are we supposed to do?"

"That's a very interesting question. I think that our tradition gives us some important guidelines. We are taught how to be genuinely and creatively present with someone in silence."

"What does that mean?"

"We wait until the mourner decides to connect with us in some way. It may be with a touch of the hand, a look or words. But we wait for them to let us know where they are at that particular moment."

"Suppose they don't say anything at all?"

"That's fine. We can sit together with them for half an hour in total silence and they will be helped by our caring presence. That is an example of true compassion."

"How can silence be compassionate? I thought that compassion only related to something you say or do."

"I believe that it goes far beyond that. The word compassion literally means to 'suffer together with,' and it reflects the highest form of being with another person. The presence of a caring, compassionate friend is the greatest gift we can bestow on another, as well as the greatest gift we can receive."

Jonathan thinks for a few minutes. "I can see that. It's hard for me to admit, but this time together with you is special to me. Our conversations are meaningful and the silent moments between us bring us even closer. But I think a lot of people just mouth the right words. They give lip service to religion."

"That's a valid point. Maybe there ought to be a Sixth Book of Moses," I reply.

"What would it contain?"

"Perhaps it could show us how to internalize and live what we learn and practice."

"I like that. A Sixth Book of Moses," says Jonathan. "Maybe then people would be more altruistic and less judgmental."

Jonathan is silent for a few moments. Then he continues, "There's a problem with not being affiliated with any group, though. I'm not even active in any clubs. What will happen to me? Is it wrong to even start thinking about my own funeral? Who will participate and what will be said?"

Chapter 14

IMAGINING A FUNERAL

I HAVE HELPED many people plan funerals. I have officiated at many of them. I don't think it is ever "wrong" to discuss such things, even when a person is perfectly healthy. Such discussions only reflect our concerns at a particular time, as well as our readiness to confront certain issues.

I am used to hearing people talk about funerals, saying things like, "What a tribute that was to Bill," or "There must have been a thousand people there." Although I have officiated at many funerals, one is especially memorable for a completely different reason.

Sylvia and Myron were a couple in their mid-sixties and I had known them casually for about 12 years. Although they were nice, they were considered a little eccentric. They were somewhat anti-social, never had many friends and were not affiliated with any synagogue or communal organizations.

When Sylvia's elderly mother became seriously ill, Sylvia asked me to visit her and I did. When her mother eventually died, Sylvia asked me to officiate at the funeral and I agreed.

On that Sunday morning, I drove to the cemetery and parked. I entered the chapel where the service was to be held at 11:00 a.m. The casket sat at the front of the room. Sylvia and Myron sat in the front pew and I went over to greet them. I spoke to the young cantor who was to co-officiate. We sat and spoke quietly for a while. Finally, I realized that even though it was almost 11:30 a.m., no one else was going to come .

The cantor and I conferred privately for a few moments. Neither of us had ever encountered anything like this before, yet we immediately agreed to proceed just as if the chapel were full.

The cantor went to the front of the chapel and began to chant the memorial prayers. He sang beautifully, with care and meaning. His tenor voice resonated throughout the chapel. When he finished, I went over to the podium and looked over at Sylvia and Myron. In my mind's eye, the chapel became filled to capacity, with an overflow crowd standing outside the door. I tried to concentrate on all that Sylvia had told me about her mother's life and incorporate those observations into my message. Somehow, I felt inspired.

When I finished, I walked over to Sylvia and Myron. Sylvia told me that while she had not been to many funerals in her life, this was the finest eulogy she had ever heard. They both told me how comforted they felt.

From that experience and many others, I have learned that there is no such thing as a "usual" or an "ordinary" death or funeral. Just as there are infinite ways to live, there are uncountable ways to pass from this world to the next. There is not a "right" way to do anything, even to die.

The importance of our lives will not be judged by the number of people who attend our funeral or even by the words that are spoken there. The significance of our lives can only be measured by what we manage to do in the time we are given – how we grow and develop. We can continue to influence ourselves, others and the world until our final breath.

"I have a little trouble with that thought."
"In what way?"

"Well, you say there is always time and for me that makes sense. After all, I've reached middle age and I'm still trying to develop my understanding of life and death. I hope that these talks with you will help me. But I've been granted more years than many others. What about people who don't seem to be given enough time? They are snatched away before they can even try to reach their potential. For me, premature death seems to be the ultimate tragedy."

Chapter 15

Premature Death

MANY OF US use the word "premature" when we really mean early. That may be because most of us share expectations of what we think of as a "normal" life span. We not only have such expectations, but we often assume we have a right to a certain number of years on this earth.

A phrase like "premature death" makes it seem as if we are in *control* of life and death. However, if death teaches us one central lesson, it is that we are truly *not* in control.

That does not mean that we must remain passive, sitting back and watching the world go by. We should make every effort to plan for the future and to do whatever is necessary for our health, well-being and security. We need to buy coats to keep us warm in winter, blankets to cover us at night, eat the right foods and exercise each day in order to stay healthy for as long as possible. However, we must also continue to grow spiritually.

It is normal to have the usual expectations of growing up, maturing and developing, getting married, raising a family, succeeding professionally and delighting in grandchildren or even great-grandchildren. It is also normal that when something prevents any of this from taking place, we are saddened and disappointed.

Death is an event our culture tries to hide and which we approach with fear and trepidation. Yet, it seems ironic that we sometimes speak of a "good" death or an "easy" passing. How can we really understand what is going on? Is a sudden death "good" because the person does not linger and suffer for a prolonged time? That may be true in some cases, but not in others. What is "good" for the patient and what is "good" for those who remain behind? I have met many people who worry about lingering too long in a helpless state, who fear having a poor quality of life and being a burden to their families. That attitude was summarized in a recent cartoon depicting one elderly man saying to another, "I hope I die before they discover something that forces me to live a really long time."

Patients express such concerns to me all the time. One woman in the final stages of terminal cancer asked me to help her. "Please," she said, "help me get ready and let me know when it's time to let go."

Everyone hopes for a "good death," although the definition of that remains ambiguous. It ultimately depends on the dynamics involved in every single relationship.

If death endows life with meaning, perhaps its most significant teaching is that life is precious. We must live in the here-and-now and also plan appropriately. We can use science for our best interests and try to eliminate pain and suffering, but ultimately, the human predicament is our unique challenge.

One day we may feel completely healthy and then, after one consultation with a doctor and perhaps some laboratory tests, we may be diagnosed with a terminal illness. One minute we may feel safe and secure, and the next, we may be the victim of a natural disaster, an accident or violence.

The more we recognize the tenuousness of life, the more easily we will approach the end of life, which *no one* can control.

Perhaps the best we can do along our journey is to approach life in a positive way, understanding that we can somehow utilize whatever happens to us along the way for our further growth and development. That is what Peter learned. His entire life became much richer and longer as a result of his "premature" illness. Peter was only 49 when he had a heart attack. That made him acutely aware of his own mortality, which now stared him in the face. But being aware of death became his salvation. He changed his entire way of eating, living, exercising and dealing with stress. His priorities shifted. I met him shortly before he died at the age of 94. He had outlived the doctors who treated him, as well as the insurers who told him he was a poor risk.

But there are no guarantees. Peter could have encountered death at any other point in his life. Few of us know when or how death will come. And we should count it a blessing that we do not know.

"We're having a philosophical discussion about the basics of life and death, which is fine and good. But the reality of my situation – of my mortality – overwhelms me at times. If I think too much about the nature of our existence, sometimes I think I'll go crazy. Maybe those who are truly psychotic have an easier time of it. After all, they don't have to deal with 'reality.' I guess I shouldn't even joke about such things. After all, my son Jeremy is not exactly mentally well. As I told you, he's been nothing but a source of pain."

Chapter 16

THE PAIN OF MENTAL ILLNESS

WHATEVER HAS CAUSED us pain throughout our lives will probably become a source of even greater pain as we or those we love approach death. Even more than physical illness, mental and emotional illnesses can create tremendous conflict for relatives of the dying.

Rachel and Robert come to mind. They are a brother and sister, aged 25 and 27 respectively, who struggled all their lives to come to terms with their mother's paranoid schizophrenia. They had no father to help them, since he died in a car accident when they were very young. Rachel and Robert were forced to cope as best they could and to grow up much faster than their peers.

"As far back as I can remember, we were always different from everyone else," says Rachel. "I used to feel so ashamed and terrified of what people might think. Sometimes Mom dressed in such a bizarre way. She'd put on too much makeup and big, floppy, frilly hats. They looked completely ridiculous on her, but she thought she looked beautiful."

"Yes," said Robert. "And then she topped all this off with pink plastic jewelry. She looked like she was playing a part in some crazy movie. Maybe that was her fantasy."

Her children often felt as if they were living in a different universe from that of their friends and classmates. "It was especially bad when Mom got off her medication," said Rachel. "The social workers tried to keep her compliant, but she was so afraid of those medicines. They had powerful side effects and she seemed more willing to feel crazy than doped up. It's so sad. She always said she loved us, but she had no idea how to be a mother. I could never invite kids home from school like everyone else. We hardly had any furniture and all of us slept on mattresses on the floor. Our refrigerator would either be empty or filled with a weird assortment of junk."

As soon as Rachel and Robert turned 18, they each took part-time jobs and moved into their own apartments. They enrolled in a local community college. As their lives became busier, they were increasingly concerned about leaving their mother alone and unsupervised. She went for long periods of time without eating or bathing. With the guidance of a social worker, they eventually placed her in a county board and care facility.

They planned to visit her regularly. However, as academic, social and other obligations mounted, Rachel and Robert visited their mother less and less. When they did go, they were depressed by her decreasing ability to carry on a rational conversation. They wondered what, if anything, their visits meant to her.

When Rachel and Robert received word that their mother was seriously ill, they did visit her, but felt they couldn't communicate with her at all. Seven months later, when she died, they were overwhelmed by all kinds of emotions. That's when they came to see me.

"I don't know how 'normal' people in 'normal' families deal with guilt," said Robert. "But Rachel and I have so much of it. I know a lot of people might think that we've been selfish all these years, thinking only of ourselves. But we honestly tried to do what was best for Mom. And if we were selfish in some ways, which we probably were, it was for our very survival. My friends all talk about the care and concern they show their parents. But their cases are different, aren't they?"

"Unless someone has been through this, they can't possibly understand," added Rachel. "Sure, I grieve for my mother and believe it or not, I will miss her. But I started grieving a long time ago for a lot of things. I grieved for the mother I never had and for the relationship that was never possible. I've tried to be a good daughter, whatever that means, but Robert and I learned a long time ago that we had to look out for ourselves. There was no one else around to be there for us."

Children inevitably experience guilt when their parents die. They typically feel, "I could have done more," or "I should have done more," remembering every wrong they ever committed and forgetting every right. Sometimes, feelings of guilt are justified and can lead to genuine remorse. Often, however, as in the case of this mother and her children, there is no one "right" answer. There is no way things can be made right for all concerned. Life is very complicated. So is death.

"I recognize that everyone has challenges and I wouldn't trade places with most people. I know mental illness is certainly as difficult as any physical illness, if not more so. It's clear that many of our gifts – and our challenges – are based on our genetic composition. It seems to me that we each have to struggle to do the best we can within our own abilities and limitations. I guess I can't complain. After all, my cousin has a kid who's severely handicapped. I don't know how they've managed to care for him all these years. And their responsibilities will never end. He's never going to grow up."

Chapter 17

A CHILD FOREVER

TO SOME EXTENT, we all remain children forever. However, as we mature into adulthood, most of us can develop our abilities to function somewhat independently in society.

However, children with developmental disabilities face particular challenges throughout their lives, as do their parents. When it comes to matters of death and dying, things become even more complicated. Many parents worry about who will take care of such a child when they are no longer around.

Henry and Julia had only one son, Albert. Julia had excellent prenatal care and was in good health throughout her pregnancy. She had an easy delivery. It soon became apparent, however, that Albert was not developing in an age-appropriate manner. The doctors never seemed to be absolutely sure about what had caused his condition, but one thing was clear. Although Albert could be educated to perform simple tasks, he would never function independently in society.

For Henry and Julia, this news was overwhelming. "I don't even know how to refer to my son," said Julia. "Years ago, we were told he was 'retarded.' In recent years, they started using terms like 'developmentally disabled.' Now it's 'developmentally challenged.' I know that they're trying to give my son proper dignity, but do the words really matter? He's never been like other kids and he never will be the same as other people his age." Henry is quieter and less willing to discuss his feelings with me or anyone. But his internal conflict and the suffering he has endured for more than half a century show clearly on his face. There is deep sadness in his eyes and his forehead is heavily lined.

These are good people and good parents who have been trying to do whatever is possible within their abilities and means. The early years were actually the easiest. "We placed Albert in special education classes or whatever they used to call them," said Julia. "We also got tutors and therapists to help him develop whatever skills he had. But, it was a hardship. Henry worked lots of overtime to be able to pay for all this."

At times, their burden seemed overwhelming. "Is it a sin to have thoughts like I sometimes had?" Henry asked in a moment of candor. "There were many times when I was sorry that Albert was born. There were actually times when I wished he would die so that our lives would be easier. Does that mean I'm a terrible person, an awful father?"

The degree of hurt and disappointment felt by Henry and Julia is impossible to quantify or express. Because of their great emotional and financial burden in caring for Albert, Julia and Henry decided not to have any more children. They were also afraid that another child might give them unforeseen problems and challenges, just as Albert had.

Like most parents, Julia and Henry tend to be self-critical, worrying that they did not do an especially good job. In truth, however, they did a very good job of allowing their son to develop to the best of his potential. They took him with them wherever they went, letting him experience as much travel and adventure as he could. As Albert grew older, however, it became clear that plans would have to be made for his future, as well as for theirs. Because they weren't in the best of health, Julia and Henry realized a time would come when they could no longer care adequately for Albert. They located a facility that provided structure, safety and a sheltered workplace. Although it was difficult for everyone concerned, they moved Albert to this rural institution when he was in his thirties and visited him often.

Unlike many people, Henry and Julia were not in denial about their own mortality. They knew that they would not live forever. They decided to make pre-need arrangements and purchase cemetery property. When they discussed their plans with me, they explained their special concerns.

"We actually need to buy *three* plots," said Julia. "Of course, we want to be buried near each other, but we've decided that we want a plot between us. That will be for Albert."

Julia's words moved me very much. Here were two aging parents contemplating not only their own mortality, but that of their child. They had made the loving decision to watch over him eternally, protecting him in death as they had in life.

"I think those people were courageous, even noble. But we're not all made of the same stuff. Sometimes the burdens of life seem too much to bear, even when you don't have certain problems. I told you about my struggle with loneliness and depression. I'm embarrassed to tell you there was even a time when I didn't think I could stand my life anymore. It's funny, because now I'm fighting to stay alive as long as possible."

"There's nothing embarrassing about having feelings, no matter what they are," I tell him. "Maybe, but I can't believe I actually once considered suicide. I'm glad I didn't go through with it, but I did think about it pretty seriously. At that time, I felt more than alone. I felt completely isolated. I didn't see any way out of my troubles.

Can you understand that?"

"Yes, I can. I know people respond to events and emotions in different ways. Depression is not something external that a person experiences. It is a deep sorrow that penetrates into your very being, into your bones, until it becomes one with you. It may even cause you to consider suicide. I would like to ask you something, though. You have often talked about the fear of being alone. What frightens you most about that?"

Jonathan looks surprised. He is quiet, lost in thought for a few minutes. "I've never really stopped to think about it. I think it's a combination of things."

"Such as?"

"Deep in the core of my being, I'm afraid I can't take care of myself."

"That's interesting. I see you as a highly intelligent scientist, someone who's very capable. In what ways do you feel you can't take care of yourself?"

"The most basic ways, emotionally and physically. I need continuous emotional support. Also I need help in shopping, cooking and cleaning."

"Has Miriam always taken care of those things for you?"

"Yeah. She knows how to deal with reality a lot better than I do."

"Is that her major role in your relationship?"

"That's a big part of it. Of course, we have a physical relationship and sometimes an emotional one, depending on how well we're communicating. Most of the time though, I feel very alone. Sometimes I'm depressed. As I told you, there have even been times when I've thought about ending it all."

Chapter 18

SUICIDE

THERE IS A natural curiosity about death. Friends and extended family often ask such things as "How old was she?" "What did he die of?" "Was it sudden?" If they feel close enough and comfortable enough to share this information, the bereaved family usually responds.

But one type of death – suicide – is often accompanied by secrecy. Some people regard taking one's own life as a supremely shameful act, even a sin. As much as possible, families try to conceal the circumstances surrounding such a death. However, by doing so, they cut themselves off from the possibility of talking about their loss with others who might bring them some comfort.

Barry's family was faced with this very dilemma. His parents and siblings had only sporadic contact with Barry after he moved to California from their home in Pennsylvania. Even though they saw each other only once a year, during the December holidays, they did maintain telephone contact.

At the age of 36, Barry learned that he had contracted a serious sexually-transmitted disease. At first, he didn't tell anyone, not even his parents. However, as his condition worsened, the changes in his appearance could no longer be camouflaged. He realized that people who were friends of his family would eventually tell them. Finally,

Barry confided in his parents. They were appalled and shocked.

Barry's closest friends seemed more accepting of his illness. Surprisingly, some continued to tell him that he was looking better, even when that was clearly not the case. They said it as if they truly believed it and perhaps they did. To Barry however, their words sounded false. He felt even more alone as a result, believing there was no one he could truly trust.

Barry felt increasingly tormented. Physically and emotionally weakened, and struggling with tremendous financial obligations, Barry saw no way out of his ordeal. He felt his family would never really understand or accept him. Sessions with a counselor did little to dissipate Barry's gloom or give him any reason to hope for anything better.

When Barry's mother came to visit, she saw signs of his depression but didn't realize the severity of it. "Of course, he was in bed most of the time and hardly talking, but the lethargy just seemed to be part of the disease."

At his request, Barry's "friends" helped him obtain and hoard a great number of sedatives. He jokingly called this secret stash his "emergency exit." Finally, one day he used it, swallowing a handful of pills and washing them down with whiskey. He went to sleep and never woke up.

His family was devastated, but they were equally distraught over what to tell people. How should they respond to inevitable questions about the death of someone so young?

I shared with them what I consider to be the most important message for families who have faced the suicide of a loved one. *There is absolutely no shame in the human struggle.* Furthermore, we need to acknowledge the suffering and pain around us. I have come to know that behind the smiling face of the woman I see on the elevator is someone who has been in despair, someone who has fantasized about taking her own life. While she can now see the events in her life from a healthier perspective, she once contemplated suicide when her physical and emotional illnesses seemed too much to bear.

We cannot judge the actions of others or condemn outright certain types of behavior. We rarely know why someone commits a particular act. For example, I have met individuals who told me that their promiscuous behavior resulted from terrible inner pain. One young man told me, "I was not trying to be promiscuous. I was lonely and looking for love."

In most cases, we truly don't know what drives someone to hasten his or her own death. In fact, after someone commits suicide, their motivation is not the central issue. Our role – as friends or relatives – is to be with the family, demonstrating our understanding and compassion as best we can. They may share with us whatever they feel is necessary and appropriate. Our mission is to be there for them, to offer our support and love during their time of loss and sorrow. As we share our best qualities, we can also share our own struggles and weaknesses. Acknowledging our own imperfections, as well as our virtues, is a gift we can bestow on others, one that can bring true comfort to a family that has been bereaved in a sudden, painful way.

"Comforting others is not always a problem for me. I think I sometimes find the right words or phrases. But afterwards, I wonder if I really believe what I've said. It's a lot harder to comfort myself, I've discovered. I can't lie to myself about all my failures and the secret humiliations that follow me as closely as my shadow. I regret all the things I've never done and may never do. At least Barry is at peace. He's crossed over to where he wanted to go. I'm glad that I've lived to see the success of the human genome project, but there are a lot of other goals I will never reach. I don't think I'll ever get to the Promised Land."

Chapter 19

THE PROMISED LAND

THE KEY TO finding self-fulfillment in life is to understand our goals and perhaps redefine and modify them as we move along. Sooner or later, we learn that *how we journey* through life is most significant. Our visions are what give us the strength to continue along our journey.

The great prophet Moses, who led the oppressed Jewish people out of Egypt, was not allowed to enter the Promised Land. However, God gave him a special gift. He showed him the Promised Land, granting him a vision of all of life until the end of days. After that, Moses was satisfied.

A vision, an understanding of the complexity of life and history, was all that was necessary to teach Moses that the goal of the journey to the Promised Land was the journey itself. That is the great lesson for us, as well. Each of us is on our own journey toward our own Promised Land. This journey is a lengthy, complex process, which requires us to continually focus on each step of the here-and-now. We are sustained during these challenging journeys by our visions.

When a couple marries, their vision is usually of special intimacy, which was well described by the 1960's singing group, the Seekers, in their song, *"I'll Never Find Another You:"*

There is always someone for each of us they say/

and you'll be my someone forever and a day/ I could
search the whole world over until my life is through/
but I know I'll never find another you.

Each partner comes into a union with special dreams and
fantasies that they hope will be fulfilled: meaningful love, satisfying
work and a loving family. These visions will lead them to many
beautiful realities. Along the way, though, the couple may face many
challenges, such as illness, disagreements and shattered dreams.

The visions that sustain a couple during these difficult moments
are renewed hopes and adjusted expectations. Their union may
become stronger as they realize they may never enter the Promised
Land. But a new vision of togetherness will be created as they
proceed along their shared journey of life.

Similarly, those who feel death approaching rely on "visions" to
sustain them, to give them hope as well as peace as they bid farewell
to their earthly existence. For a grandfather, it may be a vision of
loving grandchildren who will treasure his memory as they continue
to live in accordance with his values. For someone engaged in
communal affairs, it may be the vision of a project successfully
completed or one scheduled for future completion. For a phil-
anthropist, it may be the vision of future generations using the
hospital room, garden or playground endowed through his or her
generosity.

These are visions of self-fulfillment, of hope, of continuity and of
life. The more such visions we can create during our lifetimes, the
easier we will find it to cross over into our own Promised Land.

*"But how do we even recognize our own Promised Land? How do
we even know that we are going along our journey and not
someone else's? We're not prophets. Whose voice is going to guide
us?"*

Chapter 20

LISTENING TO OUR INNER VOICES

WHEN SOME PEOPLE approach the end of their earthly journey, they are filled with profound sadness over never having listened to their authentic, inner voices. One woman actually said to me, "I don't want to die without having lived." That same feeling, common to so many people, was summarized for me by one patient, Sonia, whose words have stayed vivid in my mind:

I am 80 years old and I have not lived my life.

When I was young, I listened to my parents.

When I was middle-aged, I listened to societal and community expectations.

When I was old, I listened to my children and grandchildren.

I never listened to my own inner voice.

Sonia said this to me as she was preparing to die. The more times we met, the more open she became in sharing her feelings and fears. During our talks, I would hold her hand and try to get her to express her own needs and desires. She began to realize that she still had the time and the power to make some important decisions on her own. That possibility excited her. One day, she said, "This is so strange, but for the first time I'm looking forward to doing something my way, even if it's planning my own funeral!"

She began to tell me details of the service she wanted, things that she had never shared with anyone. She wanted music, she told me. There was an aria from the opera *"Tosca"* that had always made her cry and she wanted others to be moved by the power of that soaring melody. And she wanted flowers, pink and purple and yellow ones. She even discussed some of her achievements that she wanted mentioned at her funeral. I felt honored that I enabled her to convey her wishes to the appropriate people.

How is it that so many people go through life without listening to their own inner voices? I see this pattern repeated over and over again. Recently, after the death of their grandfather, some grandchildren I know took their widowed grandmother out for dessert. They ordered strawberry ice cream for her, as usual.

"But I don't want strawberry," she said. "I prefer chocolate."

"How can that be, Grandma? We know that you've ordered strawberry every time for the past 50 years!"

"That was only to please your grandfather," she replied. "It was his favorite, so I felt it had to be my favorite, too."

The late Doctor Jonas Salk, who discovered the polio vaccine, spoke of finding out what "makes your heart leap." You are a unique, divine creation. Listen to your own inner voice and let it be your guide along your path.

"Do you want to hear something wonderful? I have been listening more and more to my own voice, especially during these conversations that we're having. I have also been dreaming more and trying to understand the nature of my dreams. Last night, I dreamt of Uriel again. Perhaps he is now becoming part of my inner voice, conveying what my grandfather tried to teach me. I believe that with Uriel's guidance, I am now passing through the third heaven. It is a place where I can shelter the flame of my own candle. Others may try to change its direction or even extinguish it, but there is a special place where it can endure. That brings me much comfort and solace."

First Heaven

Lighting Your Own Candle

Life on Earth

Second Heaven

Gathering the Sparks

The Present is Part of Eternity

Third Heaven

Sheltering the Flame

Protecting Your True Inner Voice

Part IV

BRIGHTENING THE FLAME

PROLOGUE

IT IS CLOSE to 2:00 p.m. on Wednesday when I next meet with Jonathan. When I enter his room, I am pleased to see that both sides of the heavy curtains are pulled back, allowing a lot of light to stream into the room. Jonathan has propped his head up on a pillow so that he can get a better view out the window.

"What are you looking at?" I ask him.

"Just one of the trees out there."

"What are you thinking about?"

"You won't believe it."

"Try me," I reply with a smile.

"I was feeling jealous of the tree."

"In what way?"

"I was looking at all those leaves bound together on that thick branch. I thought of how they're not alone. They're connected with each other."

"What does that mean to you?"

"It reminds me of how often I've felt disconnected from other people, even those closest to me."

We both become silent. Continuing to gaze out the window, we notice a large black bird sitting on the ledge outside. It is trying to open a peanut by striking it against the concrete.

102

"At least he's got something to look forward to," says Jonathan. "He's working like mad, but he'll get to enjoy the fruit of his labors. I'm happy for him. I sometimes feel that most of my struggles have been in vain."

"Could you elaborate?" I ask.

"Well, it goes back to some of the things I brought up when I first met you. When you're getting ready to die, you see things in a whole new way. Stuff that used to seem important doesn't have as much of an impact on me now. But other things do. Most of all, I'm still struggling to find the real meaning of my life. I'm just a little blip on the screen of life and then I'm going to disappear. There is no way I can even think about not being here. I'm very afraid. Maybe it serves me right. I've made other people afraid."

"In what way?"

"It's hard to describe. When Miriam and I first met, things were pretty peaceful between us and life was exciting. Our sex life was a lot better before we got married than afterwards. We seemed to be compatible in a lot of ways, trying to fulfill each other's needs. But at one point, things began to cool between us."

"What happened?"

"Well, I told you about our wedding night and my experience of Miriam distancing herself from me. I don't know if any of that is related to the way I react to her and to others. I'm not easy to get along with. I have a fairly quick temper and I can blow up pretty easily. But I say what I have to say and it's over and done with. I don't dwell on things the way that some people, like Miriam, do. Anyway, one time I was really upset about something. I can't even remember what set me off. I began yelling and screaming at Miriam and she looked at me in terror. Later, she told me that the look in my eyes reminded her of a wild animal. She cringed in fear and ran out of the room. She could never let go, never forget that one time and she never treated me the same way afterwards.

Another part of her withdrew from me. She was afraid to get too close to me or to trust me completely ever again. Maybe that's why I'm so afraid of myself, especially of my anger."

"Have you felt afraid for a long time?"

"Sometimes it seems that way. I actually was taking some anti-anxiety medication for awhile. Then I stopped. I was afraid I would become addicted to it. That's funny. In a way, even the medicine made me afraid."

"How does your fear manifest itself?"

"Sometimes in strange ways. About two years ago, I felt sure that I was in the early stages of a really nasty disease, multiple sclerosis. I started developing all the symptoms and even though I'm not a physician, I was pretty sure of my diagnosis. I was afraid to go to the doctor to have my fears confirmed."

"So what did you do?"

"Nothing. Then, one night I felt really sick. My legs felt numb. And on top of that, my heart was racing. Miriam drove me to the emergency room and they saw me right away. They didn't even make me wait. I think that made me even more afraid!"

"Then what happened?"

"Well, I was relieved, but actually a little bit embarrassed. All the tests came back negative even though what I felt was real."

"Of course it was real. It was real for you. That's what we call a 'psychic reality.'"

"But they couldn't find anything physically the matter with me. The young resident asked me if I'd been under a lot of stress recently. Stuff like that. He wondered if I'd like to be referred to a psychiatrist, but of course I refused. That would mean I had other kinds of problems, maybe even worse ones."

"Do you think you are so different from everyone else?"

"Well, I'm not sure and maybe I'm afraid to find out. It seems I'm always afraid these days."

Chapter 21
Fᴇᴀʀ

IT IS NORMAL to be afraid of the unknown. No matter what your faith, fear is a normal part of life and certainly of the dying process. Sometimes talking about your fear or anxiety with someone close can alleviate or diminish it. One patient expressed tremendous fear that he would suffer eternal damnation because he had sprayed Agent Orange during the Vietnam War. I couldn't eliminate his fears completely, but with attentive listening and by alleviating his guilt, I helped diminish his worries.

During the many years that I have counseled patients, I have discovered one very common fear relating to death. Many people have confided that they are afraid of being buried alive. One 83-year-old man, a retired business executive, was overwhelmed by such a fantasy. After all, he had seemingly been in control of matters throughout his life. How could he relinquish control for this most significant event of all?

This patient, Mr. Diskind, came up with a solution that worked well for him and his family. He made his doctor promise to have an electrocardiogram performed on him even after he was pronounced dead. He made sure that this order was placed in his medical record and that his family was made aware of his wish. For him, this plan provided the level of control, comfort and security that he required.

"I don't think my fears will be eliminated so simply. You know what's funny? Although my time is limited, I have too much time to think about the end. I keep wondering how and when it will come. Maybe they can give me something and I will just go to sleep and not wake up. I sometimes wonder if it's better just to go quickly. I must admit though, that having this time to explore my thoughts and ideas with you has been helpful. I wouldn't have had this chance if I'd died a sudden death."

Chapter 22

SUDDEN DEATH

I'VE HEARD a number of people debate the "merit" of a sudden death versus a death following a long, debilitating illness. The consensus seems to be that prolonged illness is harder for the patient, yet easier for the family. After all, they have had time to adjust to the idea of loss and to prepare themselves. By contrast, a sudden death means less prolonged suffering for the one who dies, but family and friends are left shocked and bewildered, as well as bereaved. However, just as we do not choose to be born, we rarely get the opportunity to choose the circumstances of our death.

"That's what bothers me more than anything," said Terri, a client who suffers from anxiety disorder. "All my life, I've had a vivid imagination and I've always been afraid of something bad happening to me. I keep envisioning what can go wrong and how I can be hurt or killed."

For some people, even those enjoying good health, the world may be perceived as a dangerous and unpredictable place in which the unthinkable can and does happen. The fear of experiencing harm or death may keep many people from experiencing life to the fullest.

I recently visited Renee, who was recovering from elective surgery. She was progressing nicely and her doctor had given her an encouraging prognosis. Yet, when I came into her room, I found that she was anxious and troubled.

"Is there any special reason that you're feeling like this right now?" I asked.

"I can guess," she replied. "I was just watching the news and they showed the crash of the Concorde in France. It was scary, a fiery mess. I couldn't help wondering what went through the minds of everyone on that plane. I've always been afraid to fly and this crash just heightens all my fears."

"Have you ever spoken to anyone about your fears?" I asked.

"Yeah, and I tried a couple of things but nothing seemed to work. I bought tapes and tried some relaxation training. I've read a couple of books and articles, but most of them say the same thing."

"What is that?"

"Basically, that flying is safe in comparison with all other types of transportation. But those statistics don't do a thing for me. All the experts claim that it's not really flying we're afraid of, but lack of control. I just know that I hate being in a fragile little container 30,000 feet above the ground. Anything can happen and I'm helpless to stop it. I also find myself thinking about how I'm lying here, watching this terrible news about other people. It's easy to imagine something happening to me and other people just reading about it in the paper or seeing it on TV. That's a very vivid image for me."

"Does anything besides flying make you feel the same way?"

"Yes, things like driving on the freeway and going on scary amusement park rides. And every time I hear about something bad happening to someone else, I fantasize about what it must have been like. I've always had a very active imagination."

"Is there a positive side to that?"

"Oh, I'm sure of that," Renee responded. "I'm very artistic and have gotten a lot of compliments on my watercolors. I paint beautiful things – flowers, still lifes and scenic views. My art gives me pleasure. But imagining the worst is not a great gift to have."

"What other types of situations make you imagine the worst?"

"That keeps changing, depending on what I hear about or see or read. Last year, my 25-year-old cousin was struck and killed in the crosswalk of a busy intersection. She had the green light, but a car sailed right through the red and killed her instantly. She was so beautiful and had so much to live for. She was blotted out in a moment. I'm haunted by that image."

I suggested to Renee that she might consider trying to express *all* of her emotions, including her fears, through her creativity. When we create, we become more connected with our inner selves and with others. In this way, we can become more comfortable with the human condition, including our own mortality.

Renee's fears are not uncommon. Like her, we can choose to limit our life experiences and run away from those things that frighten us. But there is another way to deal with our lack of control over the world around us. We can learn to *accept* it.

We can recognize that anything truly can happen to us at any time. Some events are more likely than others, but certainly, unforeseen events can and do occur. Our fortunes, our health and our lives can be transformed – for better or for worse – in an instant. However, if this is so, we cannot afford to take ourselves or our lives for granted. We need to continually work on ourselves in order to foster personal growth and development. Then, no matter when or how our time comes, we can find solace in knowing that we have explored ourselves and our world as best we can. We have made the most of what time and abilities we have been given.

"I know that what you describe is true. I'd like to try some new things in the time I have left. But it's one thing to talk about this stuff intellectually and another to really integrate it."

"Do you think you've made any progress in that direction?"

"Maybe."

"Would you care to elaborate?"

"Well, in our talks and in my dreams, I've seen how I've continued to grow and explore ideas. But I'm not sure what I really believe inside. Sometimes I wonder if there's a gap between the words I'm saying and what I'm really feeling. Can you understand that? Also, I'm still haunted at times by the uncertainty of it all. I still have a lot of fear. Is everyone else so afraid?"

Chapter 23

TRANSFORMING FEAR

DYING AND DEATH make many people uncomfortable and afraid. Perhaps that is because death often remains hidden away from us, taking place in sterile hospital rooms under the watchful eyes of strangers. There, patients often spend the last part of their lives on morphine drips meant to alleviate their pain. However large doses of morphine may also mean a loss of consciousness at the time of the transition from earthly life to eternal life.

Although some people prefer to die unconsciously, more and more people want to experience conscious dying. Many patients have shared this thought with me. One patient, Mrs. Sanders, expressed it best: "I was awake during all my birthday parties. I was awake for my wedding. I was awake when my children were born, when I nursed them, when they were confirmed and when they got their graduation certificates. I've been there for every significant event in my life. How can I miss this big one?"

The nurse on duty was very moved by Mrs. Sanders's words. She thought about them a great deal, especially some years later when she took care of her own sister, who was dying. She explained to her sister that if we are fortunate, we can make a choice about our final moments.

Just think about the possibility of being conscious for your ultimate union with God.

"You make it sound almost like something to look forward to. But let's be real. Pain is pretty terrible. And you can't even describe it to anyone else. Have you ever been in a lot of pain?"

"Yes, I have."

"Not just a stomachache. I mean, something really bad."

"Yes, I know what pain can be like."

"What happened to you?"

"I was in a car accident a long time ago. I needed surgery. I visit a lot of people in hospital beds, but I've also been in the bed myself."

"But now you're okay."

"More or less. I've had a lot of back pain over the years. Some other stuff too."

"Like what?"

"Kidney stones. Sometimes that pain was pretty intense."

"But you've always been able to do something for your pain."

"Mostly, yes. I try to do what I'm supposed to do. But sometimes it's been hard. And you know what I discovered? All the intellectual discussions in the world couldn't help me. I even wrote my doctoral dissertation on aspects of pain, but that didn't help me get through the hard times."

"Well, what did?"

"That's hard to say. More than anything, I think, was being able to talk on a soulful level with various professionals. Sharing words and experiences was probably what helped me the most. I ultimately tried to use my pain to become a better Rabbi, psychologist and person."

Jonathan is silent for a few moments. Then he says, "I know a lot of people want to help and they say things to try to cheer me up. But they usually say the wrong things, like, 'My aunt had the same condition and now she's better.' Or, 'You'll be better soon, don't worry.' That almost makes things worse."

"I think it's hard for people to learn to communicate on a deeper level. It takes practice to have a soulful relationship and to share your authentic self."

"But no one can possibly understand what's really going on inside me. No one can feel my pain. At this point, I can still get some relief. What will I do if the pain seems unbearable? I couldn't stand to suffer at the end."

Chapter 24

PAIN AND SUFFERING

CERTAINLY, WE ALL want to lessen the pain in our lives. But pain is not a simple thing. It is very complex, with physiological, emotional, psychological and spiritual components.

The pain before death can be exacerbated or diminished by how death is viewed. Two scholarly brothers I have known and admired, Dr. Erwin Altman and Dr. Manfred Altman, viewed death in a way that gave them inner strength and fortitude. In his memoirs, Erwin Altman wrote[2]:

> Spiritual sublimation of the pain experience needs to be rooted in the search for spiritual en-lightenment. It leads to pain not to be taken so personally, to a sharing of the pain experience with Nature and its Creator; it becomes life's greater pain as a whole. Such sharing leads to a higher threshold of tolerance of pain, as one's higher inner self is allowed to lead to the inner experience of the 'Beyond I' dimension.

This idea of identifying with and experiencing something

---

[2] Altman, Erwin. (1987). Excerpts from "Reflections on This Thing and No-Thing Called Life and Death". In *Journal of Psychology and Judaism*, edited by L. Meier. 11:2, Summer, p. 134.

infinitely greater than oneself can certainly help each of us get through periods of pain. However, it is clear that attitude and acceptance alone do not work for every person all of the time. My suggestion is that while exploring all of the pharmaceutical antidotes to pain, we should also investigate the philosophical and spiritual interventions that might help get us through these challenging times.

We are right to expect that pain can and should be diminished as much as possible. Furthermore, the careful administration of pain medication that allows us to remain conscious may enable us to truly experience the most significant moment of our lives.

For Burton, a 64-year-old man dying of kidney failure, the pain had become unbearable. He begged his doctor, "Just let me die. What's the use? It'll just get worse and worse. How much more can I take?"

Burton's doctor, an unusually kind and empathetic woman, expressed her concern for his suffering. She promised she would work together with him to alleviate his pain. Unlike some other physicians, she did not hesitate to use strong narcotics that are considered addictive. Denying them seemed absurd to her. She also suggested pastoral counseling, which is how I met Burton.

With his physician's help, Burton's pain was controlled. We were able to have conversations every day. He determined the lengths of my visit, based on his needs and strength at a particular moment. As we spoke, I saw how he was able to derive pleasure in everyday moments: seeing family members, listening to music or looking out his window at the trees in the distance. Even more important to him was the opportunity to find some meaning in his life. He began to recognize an inner spiritual dimension he had never before explored. "I've had the chance to say some things to my kids I've never been able to say before," he told me. "I think I've been a pretty good Dad. When I see my grandchildren, I can see the future. I know they'll remember me."

It is important to remember that when many patients express the desire to die, what they really are saying is that they do not want to live with so much pain.

"Well, I certainly don't want to suffer. And I hope my doctors will be able to control my pain. But as you said, there's more than the physical pain. There's the emotional pain of saying goodbye to all that I know. As much as I'd like to believe some of the things you say, I find it hard to see anything positive about the end of my life. Sometimes you make dying sound almost like a liberating experience. I wish that were true."

Chapter 25

LIBERATION

A HEIGHTENED AWARENESS of mortality and dying can actually be liberating. It can promote our growth and deepen our relationships. But before things get better, they sometimes get worse.

Whatever has affected us throughout life – anxiety, depression, compulsive behaviors, rage or any neurosis – may intensify during a final illness. This pattern applies even more so to severe pathologies, such as borderline personality disorder and psychosis.

Also, certain family issues, such as marital discord, do not disappear at the time of impending death. Sometimes matters that have lain dormant for years arise anew, with more intensity than ever. One 69-year-old man who knew that his death was near spoke to me about his wife of 35 years. "She doesn't care about me at all. She doesn't care if I die."

When I asked him to elaborate, he said, "Right before they brought me into the hospital, I was having a pretty severe attack and I could hardly breathe. I asked her to get my medication for me and she said she couldn't find it. Can you imagine not being able to find my nitroglycerin pills after 35 years of marriage?"

Nothing is ever as simple as it seems. When I spoke to this man's wife, I learned something very interesting. Almost 15 years earlier, her husband had betrayed her by having an affair. After he had tearfully apologized and promised that it would never happen again, she took him back and they never spoke of it. Yet clearly, some intense anger remained. Could she really not find his medication or did she secretly prefer him dead? Her husband seriously considered calling his attorney to his hospital room and rewriting his will to deprive his wife of part of her inheritance. This would be his way of punishing her for her callousness and betrayal. However, he eventually realized that his vengeful feelings were based on false assumptions. He reconsidered and decided not to change his will.

Sometimes, impending death can bring out the best in people. It can actually liberate us from the challenges of coping with life and all its expectations.

A dying patient once "confessed" to me: "I don't have to prove anything to anyone. I can finally be myself." One prominent professor who was dying felt unusually relaxed, as he told me, "I don't have to pay homage to the goddess of success. What a great feeling!"

A different sort of liberation was described by a 57-year-old man who found himself suddenly suffering from cardiac failure. He told me that he had been going out with the same woman for eight years but had never wanted to commit to marriage. Now, he finally decided to get married. Suddenly, all his prior fears and doubts vanished. Overnight, he had become a risk-taker and he found the experience liberating. He summoned a justice of the peace to his hospital room and in a brief but moving ceremony, the couple was wed.

If I were to suggest a little rule of thumb, it is this: as you have lived, so will you die. Learn to draw, appreciate music, develop relationships with people and God and make the world a better place for tomorrow. There is always time for this – until you draw your final breath. Then, when your time comes, you will not be so afraid. Death will simply be your final stage of growth.

"You seem to be saying that I can come to terms with death and it can even be a liberating experience. But how can I feel liberated from some of the really bad stuff I've done? I've told you about my anger. There's other stuff. The more we speak, the more I realize how often I never really communicated with Miriam. She didn't seem to understand me and I kept a lot of stuff bottled inside. Here I was, with a wife and family, but I still felt lonely inside. When I finally found someone I could really talk to, I did something..."

"What happened?"

Jonathan sighs before speaking again. "I haven't always been a faithful husband. About ten years ago, I went to an out-of-state convention with a female colleague. We spent a lot of time together and we ate all our meals together. We had great conversations. She was a joy to talk to and she seemed to really understand me. It was real emotional intimacy. I was feeling more and more visible to her. When I talked to her, I felt less alone. One thing led to another and we ended up having an affair. Miriam found out about it, but she took me back. She said she forgave me, but I sometimes wonder if she could just forget about it. Sometimes I feel guilty."

Chapter 26
GUILT

GUILT IS A universal feeling. It is usually based on how we feel about things we did or did not do. It is not necessarily a bad thing, since it is a natural consequence of living. At some point in our lives, each of us may have to confront physical, mental or emotional illness. How we respond to these defining moments may produce guilt as well as other feelings. But this guilt may be healthy or pathological, depending on its underlying cause, frequency, intensity and duration.

Everyone has some guilt. People often want to talk about their "guilty feelings" when they sense their end is near. I hear so many stories, so many confessions, and each individual feels that he or she is the only one who has ever had such a thought or committed such an act.

Walter, who was terminally ill, told me he believed his illness was a punishment of some sort. When I asked him to elaborate, he said: "Rabbi, you don't understand. I'm a fraud. Most of the really important things in my life I've gotten through cheating. Even my diploma is worth nothing. I bought it from a mail-order place about twenty years ago, when I needed something to hang on my wall. I've even put phony awards and achievements on my resume to make it look better. I was so good at fooling people that one community group even honored me last year as an outstanding citizen."

As we continued to talk, Walter gained some insights into the reality of his life. True, he had misrepresented himself, but over the years he had proven himself to be a very capable businessman. He had built up his company almost single-handedly, demonstrating that he really was good at what he did. His natural talents and abilities had enabled him to prosper. No one could take that away from him.

Walter was not perfect. No one is. As long as we live, we continue to err. However, when we make mistakes, we can learn how to rectify them and even how to grow from them.

"But I told you, I've done some things with terrible consequences. Even though my wife told me that she shared responsibility for some of what went wrong and she forgave me for many things, she never forgot them. Is it ever possible to really forgive?"

Chapter 27

FORGIVENESS

DYING PEOPLE, perhaps more than any others, recognize the need for forgiveness. They see the totality of experience, including birth and death, health and illness, and wealth and poverty. They can better understand the indiscretions of other people and their narcissism. They are therefore more able to forgive others who may have strayed from the ethical or moral path. They may even be willing to relate to people they have come to hate.

People eventually discover how liberating forgiveness can be. They forgive for their own sake, rather than only for the sake of others. They thus free themselves from the burdens of bitter memories, score-keeping and animosity that have weighed them down throughout the years.

It is also important to learn how to forgive oneself – for past indiscretions, poor judgment, having acted in a selfish way, being controlling or for just being human and fallible.

One healthy, vivacious woman I know was working as a successful family law attorney when she was diagnosed with a brain tumor at the age of 50. Fearing the worst, she thought she had only a few months to live. Fortunately, her tumor turned out to be benign and she is completely healthy once again. But her life has been changed forever.

When she believed she faced imminent death, she sought forgiveness in the most important area of her life. She asked her husband to forgive her for taking him and their marriage for granted. As she put it, "Please excuse me for being nice to my clients and moody to you. My scare woke me up."

Her husband forgave her and their marriage is now far happier than it was before.

I hope each of us can learn to discern the real nature of things while we are still healthy. Think about this today.

"You're telling me that there's still time to set some things straight, even between me and Miriam, even between me and Jeremy."

"What do you think?"

"I'd sure like to believe that it's possible. But I don't know if I can do it in time. There's so much to talk about, so much to try to understand. And I'm not sure I have the courage or the strength necessary to get to that place. Or if I can change the course of anything."

"What makes you say that?"

"I think it might be because...because of all my guilt. I'm so scared. I'm afraid because I've done so many bad things. Maybe that's why I'm sick now. I can't help feeling that I'm responsible for some of the hardships in my life."

Chapter 28

CAUSE AND EFFECT

MOST OF US look for neat solutions in life, trying to find clear links between cause and effect. Particularly during hard times, such as illness, we tend to ask a lot of questions of ourselves. Why are we experiencing pain and suffering? What have we done to deserve this? Is this a form of punishment for our sins or a consequence of our behavior? Suppose we have not actually acted in a bad way, but have thought something really terrible, so shameful that we cannot share it with anyone else?

I hear these questions almost daily as I visit people who are confronting very difficult situations. Many people seem to feel that life can be summarized as "I did X and therefore Y happened." However, this approach proves most unsatisfactory when someone is facing illness, especially serious illness. The universal questions of every patient, spoken or unspoken, are: "Why me? Why now?" The answers are never easy, yet people try to find them.

Randy, a 57-year-old, thought he found a simple answer to these questions, but they turned out to be more complex than he imagined. He had checked into the hospital for planned abdominal surgery. He spoke with me the day before the operation. He admitted that he had never taken adequate care of his body. In fact, he had regularly abused it. He smoked. He had been grossly overweight for most of his life and even though he had shed some pounds before the surgery, his excess weight still made him a surgical risk. "So you see, Rabbi, I'm to blame. I brought this on myself," he said. "I'm just getting paid back for all the bad stuff I've done. Maybe unconsciously I was killing myself."

As we continued to talk, I conveyed my feelings that things are not usually that simple or clear-cut. I wished Randy well and promised to visit him daily. Later that night, something extraordinary happened. At 8:30 p.m., Randy suffered a heart attack. Since he was in the hospital as a pre-surgical patient, he was already on an intravenous drip and a heart monitor. He received immediate expert intervention and the doctors stabilized him fairly quickly. Several days later, one of them told him, "You're really lucky you were already in the hospital. I think that saved your life." Suddenly, Randy began to reassess his view of the world. He realized his life, like every other, is quite complex. His planned surgery, which he regarded as a punishment, actually saved his life. Instead of a curse, it was a blessing. Randy still has to wrestle with the forces that drive him to self-destructive behavior, but he is trying his best to understand his illness and himself.

He is not the only one who has spent long hours in introspection, searching for answers. I recently visited Tony, a 49-year-old man battling a particularly difficult form of cancer. He is very thoughtful and bright. His marriage of ten years ended two years ago and he has no children. His one sister visits him frequently, offering whatever moral support she can.

During our talk, Tony seemed quite depressed. Several times he appeared to be on the verge of saying something, but he held back. Finally, just as I was about to leave his room, he said, "I think I know why this happened to me."

"You do?" I replied. "What do you think?"

"I figured it out," he said. "You know, I've told you about my Mom, how she's gotten weaker and weaker. She's been in a nursing home for the past two years and it costs a fortune. She and Dad worked hard and saved all their lives to build up some decent savings. And now, as I watch this money just drain away for her care, I can't help thinking that there won't be much left for me and my sister. And I could really use the money now. I actually made a kind of mental 'deal' a few months ago. I thought, 'If she's going to die anyway, please take her now. It will be better for her and for me.' I was really bargaining her life away. Can you imagine a son doing such a thing? Is it any wonder I got sick?"

Tony did not realize that this was certainly not the first time I heard such a "confession," such a response to the eternal questions: "Why me?" and "Why now?"

I do not have simple answers for people like Tony. I grapple with the same questions of life, suffering and death as everyone else. The most honest response I can give is to share my own struggles, my doubts and my victories. After Tony and I spoke for a while, I returned to my office on a different floor of the hospital. But about fifteen minutes later, I suddenly decided to return to Tony's room. I went in, took his hand and held it. Neither of us spoke, but I could feel Tony relaxing. At that moment, all I could offer him was my unequivocal support. All I could do was be there for him and he sensed that.

Through the silence, unspoken messages were conveyed. We are all fallible. We sometimes think and do things we are ashamed of. But we are not score keepers and ultimately we cannot understand all the workings and mysteries of the universe.

In this world, we can only surmise, we can only question, we can only ponder and attempt to come up with answers that may work for us throughout our lives and in the face of death.

"*This is the sort of story I relate to. When I hear about someone who's thought the unthinkable, it makes me realize that maybe I'm not the only one who does that. I still don't know if I completely believe all of the things we're talking about, like angels for example. But who knows? Perhaps Uriel is really guiding our discussion. Maybe my grandfather is, too. So far, it seems as if everything we've talked about – or that Uriel has led us to talk about – involves what it means to be human. I have a sense I may be passing through the fourth heaven. Perhaps in order to ascend to a higher level, we first have to acknowledge that we make mistakes. We think and do wrong things. Our feelings and desires pull us in different directions. But as long as we look for ways to correct the past and continue our spiritual growth, we are still headed in the right direction.*"

First Heaven

Lighting Your Own Candle

Life on Earth

Second Heaven

Gathering the Sparks

The Present is Part of Eternity

Third Heaven

Sheltering the Flame

Protecting Your True Inner Voice

Fourth Heaven

Brightening the Flame

Accepting Being Human

Part V

ILLUMINATING THE WAY

PROLOGUE

ON THURSDAY, Thanksgiving, around 3:00 p.m., I come to the hospital to take care of a few matters. Once there, I find a message on my voice mail from Jonathan saying he would like to speak to me.

When I enter Jonathan's room, I notice that once again the curtains are pulled back. Even the sheer curtain has been drawn back so that we can see clearly through the window. Intense light streams into the room.

A nurse is attending to Jonathan as I enter. She is adjusting the line of his I.V. and monitoring its flow. She asks Jonathan if he is comfortable. When he nods that he is, she smiles at him warmly and touches her hand lightly to his forehead. She smiles at me and quietly leaves the room.

"What's on your mind?" I ask Jonathan.

"I'm not sure," he says. "I've been thinking about a lot of different things. Maybe it's because of Thanksgiving. Almost everyone who works here has somewhere else to go this evening, but I'll just be here. It sure doesn't feel very festive. I did get a card, though," he says, showing me a hand-made drawing of a turkey, with a get well message inside.

"Who gave you that?" I ask.

"It's funny, but I'm not really sure. A couple of teenagers stopped by and told me they were visiting from their school, but I didn't even catch the name of the place. They said 'get well soon' and gave me this card and then wished me a happy Thanksgiving. It was sweet of them. I was glad they stopped by, even for a few minutes. I guess it's their good deed for the day and then they go home and join their families for dinner. What about you, Rabbi? How are you doing? You look a little different today. Preoccupied. Is everything okay?"

I hesitate a moment before replying. "Well, truthfully, Thanksgiving is always a challenging day for me."

"Why is that, Rabbi, if you don't mind my asking?"

"I don't mind. Thanksgiving has a number of associations for me. Some are pleasant, while others are sad."

"To quote you, 'Would you like to elaborate?'"

I laugh. "I see you know how to draw me out. Let me tell you a little bit about me and Thanksgiving. First of all, it was my father's favorite holiday and I have a lot of fond childhood memories of our special meals together."

"Can you tell me a little bit about your father?"

"Yes. He was a happy, kind and gentle man. I think that was his greatest legacy to me. He used to enjoy helping my mother cook, particularly for holidays. I can still picture him in the kitchen, helping get the Thanksgiving turkey ready."

"Was it just you and your parents?"

"No, I have a brother. And my grandfather lived with us, too."

"You must have had a big place."

"Actually, we didn't. It was a small apartment in New York, but my father made sure there was always room for his father there, too."

"Your father sounds like a nice guy. But you're talking about him

in the past tense. He's no longer alive?"

"That's correct. And do you know when he died?"

"I can guess from your tone of voice. On Thanksgiving?"

"You're a hundred percent right. His death always affects how I feel on this holiday."

"How old were you when it happened?"

"I was just 26. I was already married and had just become a father myself. So I experienced great joy and great sorrow at the same time. It feels as if it happened yesterday."

"So you're thinking about him today?"

"Absolutely. I think about my father very often, but especially on Thanksgiving. This holiday is always a little bittersweet for me."

"I appreciate your telling me about that. Now I feel a little more connected with you. Also, I noticed that while we were talking about your father, I was focusing less on myself. I forgot some of my pain for awhile. I sometimes forget that you have feelings, too. When I see other people going in and out of here, I sometimes actually believe they live a different kind of life. They seem not to have any cares or worries. They just come here and do their job and go home. I know that can't be so, but it sure seems like it. Especially the doctors. They seem so in control. They're always racing from one place to another. They're so busy. I don't think they're ever allowed to get sick."

"Do you really believe that?" I ask.

"Of course not, but they do seem invulnerable."

"Would it surprise you to know that many of the physicians you see have been patients here, too?"

"I imagine that's true, but when I see them running from room to room, it's hard to picture."

"You describe that very well. I sometimes also have to remind myself about what really goes on here. This is a place where those

who are temporarily sick are taken care of by those who are temporarily well. Sometimes we trade places."

"It must be hard for doctors to be patients."

"I think it is. It's a great adjustment and sometimes knowing too much can cause them a lot of concern. But a number of doctors have told me they've grown from the experience. They've become more empathetic and they now have a better understanding of what patients go through."

"I don't really have that much contact with my doctors. They come by really early in the morning. We talk a bit and they leave orders. But it's the nurses who really take care of me. They're the ones I get to know, a little bit anyway."

"How have they been treating you?"

"They've been really good to me. You just saw Irene. When she's on duty, she really makes my day. She goes the extra mile. It's not so much what she does, but how she does it. We sometimes talk about other things, too. She's from the Philippines and she helps out her relatives who are still there."

"How about some of your other care givers?"

"I'm pretty satisfied. Some take more time to talk to me than others. Some make me feel more comfortable. There is one technician who draws my blood almost every day who has a nice gentle touch. When she can't find a vein right away, she feels so bad. She hates to have to stick me again."

"Do they have a lot of problems getting into a vein?"

"Well, sometimes. I think I've got thick skin."

We both laugh and I say, "Can you tell me what you really mean by that?"

"I get it. You're being a shrink. You want me to analyze why I said that, don't you? Well, it's true. I've developed a thick skin over the years. You have to in order to make it through life. If you don't,

you'll let everything get to you. You've got to protect yourself. There's a limit to how much you can share with others. I'm surprised I'm even sharing this with you."

"Well, I'm happily surprised," I reply.

He smiles, then continues. "Anyway, I was telling you about the help here. One of the aides has been especially kind. I was scared the other night and didn't want to be alone. He stayed with me until I felt better and he came back to check on me later.

"You won't believe this, Rabbi, but I think one of the best healers around here is the woman who comes to clean my room and bathroom every morning. She comes in so early to do the job, but she's always in a good mood. She doesn't speak much English, but she always says 'Good Morning' with a smile and sometimes hums a pleasant tune. She cheers me up. I think she changes my mood as much as some of my pills do. I actually envy her sometimes. She knows how to enjoy life.

"I couldn't do a lot of the things some of these people do. They change my gowns and dressings, clean me up and empty my urinal. Others take samples of my bodily fluids to send to the lab. They're not disgusted by the way I look or by anything that comes out of my body."

"Do you really think that anything about your body is disgusting or shameful?" I ask. "We've already talked about how there's no shame in being human. That includes having a body, which is a holy vessel for the soul and is worthy of respect."

"Intellectually, I can see that. But on a daily basis, I can't help feeling a lack of dignity. I'm exposing parts of myself to others that I never have before. At times, I'm overwhelmed by feelings of helplessness. If it weren't for these special people, I don't know what I'd do. Maybe they're angels?"

Chapter 29

ANGELS

MANY ANGELS live among us. Some "work" for terminally ill patients. They may receive a salary, but that is never their primary motivation.

A physician I know, Dr. W., was a true angel of mercy for one of her patients, an 85-year-old man from Buenos Aires. As his disease progressed and he knew that his death was near, Carlos felt that he could tell his caring doctor his secret wish: he wanted to go home to die. He couldn't imagine dying in Los Angeles, far from his roots and his extended family in Argentina. Dr. W. listened closely to what Carlos was saying. He had been her patient for a long time and she had come to care deeply for him. She knew he had no one to accompany him on his journey home, so she thought about what she could possibly do to make his wish come true.

The more she thought about it, the clearer the answer became: she would travel with Carlos. It wasn't a simple decision. "I felt torn," she later told me. "I have many other patients to consider and of course, I've got my husband and children to think about as well. But it was just the right thing to do." Without telling her friends or associates about her mission, Dr. W. took "vacation" time and bought a ticket for the long flight to Buenos Aires. She traveled the whole way with Carlos and stayed long enough to help him get settled in his family's home. I believe she served as a healing messenger for him.

These angels in our midst begin their service as strangers, but eventually each becomes an *Anam Cara*,[3] a soul friend.

"I agree that someone like Dr. W. is truly special. I'm lucky in some ways. I've got a good relationship with my doctor, my nurses and with you. But even with the best of medical and nursing care, I have to tell you that I sometimes feel lonely and scared. I feel so unprotected. I wake up anxious."

I respond, "I can understand that. We've talked about how we need mothers and other nurses throughout our lives. I think we also need another type of caregiver – a midwife. By that I mean a special person who can help us spiritually during the defining moments of our lives."

---

[3] *Anam Cara*: A Book of Celtic Wisdom, by John O'Donohue. N.Y. Cliff Street Books, 1997.

Chapter 30

MIDWIFE

WE EXPERIENCE a number of birthing processes throughout our lives. Each of these requires the assistance of a midwife. Most lifetimes contain at least three momentous birthing experiences: when we are physically born, when we get married and when we die.

Every woman who gives birth recognizes the importance of a midwife. That special person may be a nurse, physician or close friend who helps her stay psychologically, emotionally and physically centered during the birthing process.

As we discussed earlier, often before a couple gets married, one of them experiences significant anxiety. They may even consider postponing or canceling the wedding. I know of a few cases where this actually happened the night before the ceremony. At times like that, sometimes a "midwife" appears – a dear soul friend, an *anam cara,* who helps the bride or groom breathe, calm down and walk down the aisle. That person's healing presence helps eliminate the tension and stress for the bride or groom.

The same type of process takes place when someone is dying. At that time, the "midwife" helps the dying person prepare to move beyond the threshold of this life.

I remember being at the bedside of a dying man who had been religious throughout his lifetime. As he lay there, surrounded by his wife, children and grandchildren, he began to say things that his family had never heard before. He began to express his fears and his doubts about his religious ideology, including the concept of life after death. His wife looked horrified, fearful that he had uttered blasphemous thoughts. She blurted out, "You don't really mean that. You don't know what you're saying."

I took the man's hand and looked into his eyes. "I have doubts also," I said softly. "I am also afraid. But that's okay. We are allowed to be human." I continued to hold his hand and he looked noticeably more relaxed.

While serving as midwives, we do our best to be there for the dying person. But we cannot always be there. At times, the person may choose to remain alone. The physical presence of another person is not always required. An image or memory of someone special may suffice to make the transition easier. For example, many dying people are comforted by one of their earliest images and memories – the face of their mother. When they see her clearly and cry out "Mama," she becomes a psychic midwife in their re-birthing process.

"I like the image of being reborn. But I think that one of the most frightening things about dying is that ultimately we have to do it alone, no matter who is with us at our bedside. No other person – a midwife or anyone else – can go with us. Even you can only accompany me so far. After that, I will be all alone."

Chapter 30

BEING ALONE

BEING ALONE is actually our natural state. Our path through life is a lonely one, although along the way there may be wonderful moments of togetherness. Sometimes loneliness and togetherness actually co-exist, occupying the same time and space.

Think about a wedding and the emotions of the bride and bridegroom. As they come together, they are still two unique individuals who are each on a solitary journey of personal experience and growth. At the time of the wedding, however, their aloneness is mitigated by the presence of family and friends, while music, dancing and other festive touches create a feeling of togetherness.

We also feel alone when we are ill, even if we're surrounded by physicians, nurses, social workers and clergy. Each of us is on a solitary journey, not only physically but psychically, a voyage that reflects our personal uniqueness. Ultimately, we know we will die alone. No one can accompany us on our unique voyage.

However, death can be a great teacher. It can show us the need to accept aloneness as an important aspect of life, as well as of death. It challenges us to live comfortably in our solitude.

No matter how close the relationship may be between husband and wife, brother and sister, teacher and student, or doctor and patient, each of us goes through life essentially alone. Jens Peter Jacobsen suggested a beautiful understanding of aloneness[4]:

> It was the great sadness that a soul is always alone.
> Any belief in the merging of one soul with another is
> a lie. Not the mother who took you onto her lap, not
> a friend, not the wife who rested next to your heart...

Solitude allows us the opportunity to have a dialogue with all the different parts of our self, to get in touch with all aspects of our being and to hear our authentic inner voice. Being alone is the most effective way to get to "know thyself." Rainer Maria Rilke even suggested that solitude is essential to know oneself[5]:

> What is necessary, after all, is only this: solitude, vast
> inner solitude. To walk inside yourself and meet no
> one for hours – that is what you must be able to
> attain.

Creativity can be enhanced through solitude. I know a fine painter, Amy, who owns a small home in the mountains near Lake Arrowhead, north of Los Angeles. Every summer, she retreats to that dwelling for a few weeks. During that time, she rises early, goes for long walks and savors the natural beauty around her. Most of her time is spent in solitary contemplation: thinking, imagining and visualizing.

"When I return, I feel so refreshed, so renewed," Amy has told me. "People often ask me where I get my imagery or my colors or my subjects. The truth is that during those weeks I get enough inspiration to keep me going for the rest of the year. If I didn't have

---

[4] Jacobsen, J.P. *Niels Lyhne*. Translated from the Danish by Tiina Nunnally. Seattle: Fjord Press, 1990, p. 203. Originally published in 1880.

[5] Rilke, R. M. *Letters to a Young Poet*. translated with a forward by Stephen Mitchell. New York: Vintage Books, 1984, p. 54. Originally written in German 1903-1908.

other obligations, I would try to spend even more time alone throughout the year."

It is only when we do not appreciate the gift of solitude that we begin to experience a negative type of aloneness – loneliness. Yet even in this loneliness, which at times feels like alienation and isolation, we can also find an understanding of the "loneliness" of God, as it were. A friend once told me that while she was lighting the Sabbath candles, she sensed this loneliness of God and wished God a "Good *Shabbos*." This mutual loneliness of man and God was beautifully expressed by a dying friend, Dr. Erwin Altman, who wrote in his journal[6]:

> I am dying alone, as nobody can accompany me, where I am going, I am "on my own," as never before in my life. But just in this "alone-ness," which I am facing now, I am closer to God's identity and His alone-ness than ever before. In this true alone-ness I experience and recognize my own very Divinity from within the Image of God.

"I can understand the need for solitude at times. But I have to tell you that the way I'm feeling now, I need to have someone else around, someone I can talk to about what really matters to me without embarrassment or shame. I guess I need you to be my friend."

---

[6] *Ibid.*, Altman, p. 137.

Chapter 32

FRIENDS

WE ALL NEED friends to help us get through life, particularly during the challenging times. I once visited a patient who turned out to be someone I had known since high school. Over the years we had gone our separate ways, leading very different lives in different communities. Objectively speaking, we seemed to have little in common. Yet somehow, the fact that we shared memories of teachers and homework assignments and had visited each other's homes created a special bond between us. After I spent a few minutes in his room, this man opened up to me and spoke with great feeling as he shared the most intimate aspects of his life.

Perhaps you have had a similar experience. One woman told me about a childhood friend whom she has known since the age of 11. Even though they only see each other once every 10 years, as soon as they meet they can speak with each another in an intimate, relaxed way, as if no time at all has passed since their last meeting.

This is often the case with a person who has shared the early part of your life. Such friends may have been classmates, visited your childhood home or may have known your parents or grandparents. These early bonds can last a lifetime.

Sometimes you can form a deep attachment to another person very quickly. You recognize some spark of yourself – perhaps a shared view, a preference or a sense of humor – and you feel that you can trust that person with your deepest secrets.

Such soul friends are extremely important in life and also in the dying process. Soul friends provide a comfort zone for the spirit in an otherwise seemingly indifferent world.

One woman told me that while driving to her father's funeral with a good friend of hers, they passed a park where she saw some young boys playing basketball. She thought, "How can they play ball when my father just died?" Then she turned to her soul friend in the car, whose presence provided comfort and a world of healing for her.

Sometimes you feel closer to a soul friend than to a family member. With a soul friend, you can comfortably share anything, even frailties, fears and vulnerabilities you might hide from your family.

That is why a soul friend is especially important when a person is facing death. Very often, the family creates an atmosphere of denial around the patient. I remember vividly one wonderful encounter I had with a 77-year-old man who was dying. I entered his hospital room, not knowing how long the visit would last or if he would even be receptive to me. But this gentleman shared a great deal with me. He opened up about his wartime experiences, his losses and his regrets. His eyes began to well with tears. Just as he was about to reveal something very significant, there was a knock at the door. His daughter entered the room, carrying a box of pastries that she had picked up from the bakery. "Look, Daddy, I got your favorite Danish!" she said.

The atmosphere of the room shifted dramatically. The patient was careful to control himself as he smiled at his daughter and welcomed her. He clearly wanted me to stay, but felt unable to continue with the themes he had begun. He felt ashamed to continue this conversation in front of his daughter. She was trying her best to cheer him up. In an instant, the conversation had shifted from existential matters to a discussion of which bakery in town makes the best Danish.

I don't fault his daughter for acting as she did. Most families enact a similar charade when a relative is seriously ill or dying. They do not feel comfortable addressing the reality of the situation. As a result, however, they miss out on glorious opportunities to communicate on a far deeper level than ever before. They lose the chance to give one another the greatest gift possible. By acknowledging that someone is dying, we enable that person to get the most out of the time that remains.

Certainly, however, we need to take into account how information is shared. Our choice of words becomes particularly crucial. We have to be careful to always allow for some form of healing. Our goal is to be with others as fully and authentically as we possibly can.

The presence of a soul friend is invaluable. Throughout your life, try to develop as many soul friends as you can. When you approach death, they will help bring you peace and comfort.

"I don't know if I'll have time to make new soul friends. The people who actually seem to comfort me are the staff people I told you about, folks I haven't known for very long. They're not old friends, but a group of strangers."

Chapter 33

THE STRANGER

IN MANY STORIES in the Bible, a "stranger" plays a pivotal role. Very often, someone whose name is not even recorded does something so significant that it changes the entire course of history.

This pattern is true in our lives as well. Sometimes, a person appears – seemingly out of nowhere – to help us through a time of challenge or transition. Charlotte told me how when she was a hospital patient, a new nurse came on duty for the night shift. She was especially kind and took the time to talk and listen to Charlotte, who was feeling particularly vulnerable and scared. The nurse even gave Charlotte a relaxing massage that helped her sleep.

When you are in a hospital, you are surrounded by strangers. But each of them may share a special moment with you, as if they were sent for just that purpose. As you are being taken for a test in a wheelchair or on a gurney, the woman transporting you may sense that you are cold and put an extra blanket on your lap. The man who comes to bring your food may smile and ask about you in such a caring way that your entire day is brightened.

Transitions in life require the assistance of other people. For many at the end of life, the most amazing part of giving birth to oneself spiritually is being assisted by nurses and other midwives who are complete strangers. We share the most intimate aspects of our bodily functions and soulful experiences with people we do not know.

At these moments we realize that there is something very special about these strangers, who may be from a different culture, religion or race. They remind us that we are all one.

One woman told me that before her hospitalization, she had stereotypes of certain ethnic groups and was even hostile toward men. Yet, during the course of her illness, she was attended to by strangers from the very ethnic groups that she used to look down on. She also found that most of her care givers were kind, comforting men. All these strangers helped her discover a new part of herself, enabling her to see the world with greater clarity and love. She found that when strangers touch your heart, you are able to grow and develop your character and other parts of yourself. In this way, you become more fully alive.

Helpful strangers represent the strongest bond of all – the unique commonality of being human, with all of its frailties and privileges. These strangers are often our angels, the special messengers sent by God, as we have already discussed.

"Maybe I'm more comfortable with the notion of angels than I used to be. In my dreams and even when we speak, I've continued to hear the voices of my grandfather and of Uriel. I think what they're conveying to me now is that I am surrounded by angels even while I'm still within my body. Perhaps I am passing through the fifth heaven, recognizing that there are angels in my midst."

First Heaven

Lighting Your Own Candle

Life on Earth

Second Heaven

Gathering the Sparks

The Present is Part of Eternity

Third Heaven

Sheltering the Flame

Protecting Your True Inner Voice

Fourth Heaven

Brightening the Flame

Accepting Being Human

Fifth Heaven

Illuminating the Way

Angels on Earth

Part VI
LIGHTING THE NEXT CANDLE

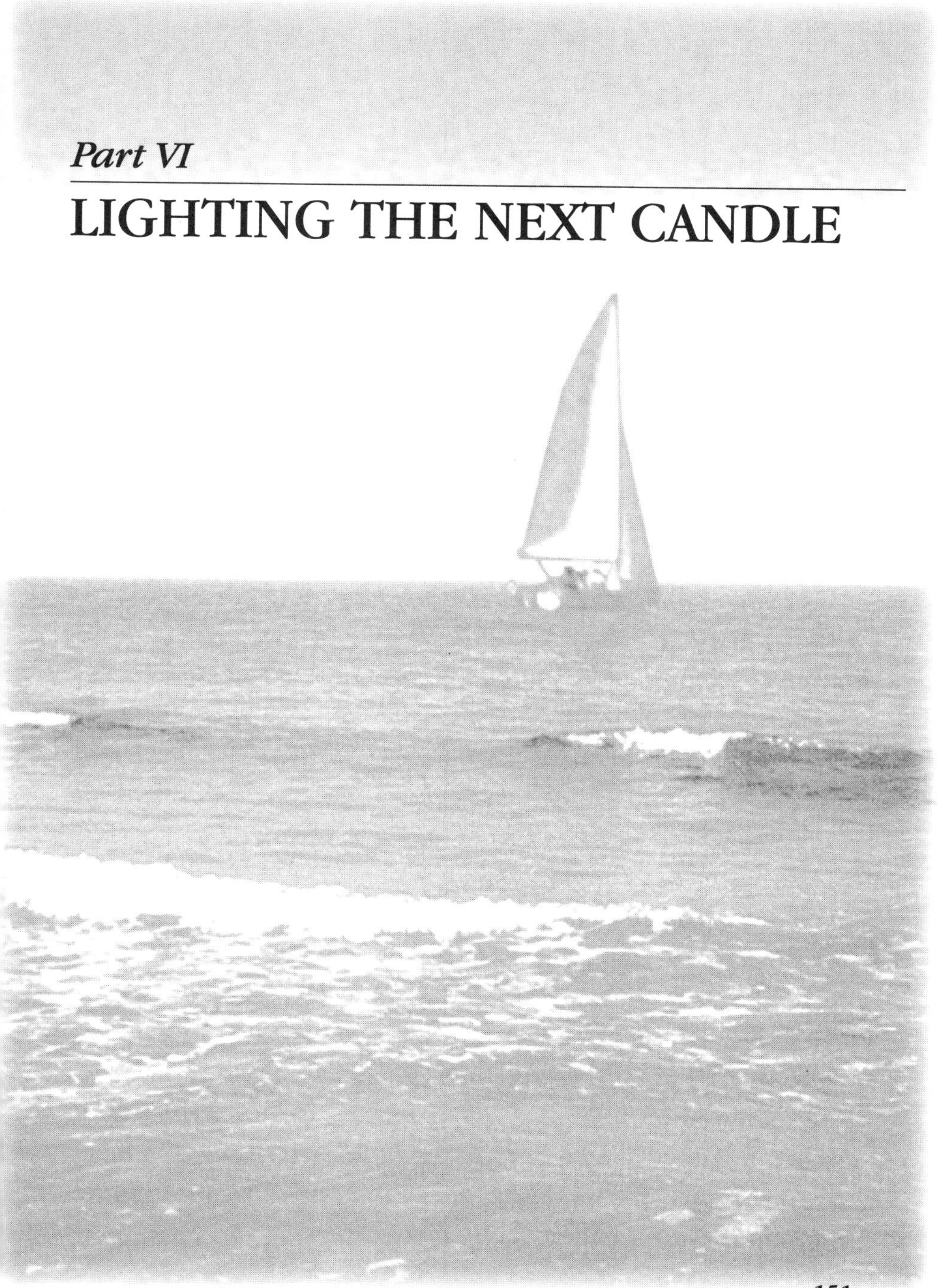

PROLOGUE

IT IS FRIDAY afternoon, close to 3:00 p.m. Jonathan has asked me to stop by again. He has surprised me with an unusual request. He watched our pre-Sabbath video and has decided he would like some electric Sabbath candles for his room. I bring a set with me.

As I enter Room 5947, I am struck by how bright it appears. All the curtains have been pulled back so that we can see clearly through the windows. I ask Jonathan where he'd like me to put the candles.

"I'd ask you to put them right next to the bed but I'm afraid their light will shine into my eyes. How about over there on the window sill? I'll be able to see them but they won't be so intrusive."

I plug them in where Jonathan has suggested and make sure the bulbs are working. "Was there any special reason you requested these?" I ask him.

"I'm not sure. We've been talking a lot about light. My mother used to light candles when I was a kid, but I haven't seen it done in years. My wife was never into that and I guess I didn't care much, either. But light is comforting, as I'm noticing more and more. And I enjoyed watching your wife light the candles in the video. I wish I could have real candles in here, but I know I can't because of safety regulations. I don't want to set the place on fire!"

"I appreciate that," I tell him.

We both laugh. "Are you sure we're allowed to joke in a place like this?" he asks.

"I can't think of any reason not to. For me, it's one of the great pleasures in life. What about you?"

"I used to have a great sense of humor. But I haven't found much to laugh about lately."

"I can understand that. But is there anything that brings you pleasure?"

He hesitates. "I suppose so. I liked watching the video and listening to the songs. The tape brought back some memories and they were good ones. I even recognized one melody. It was 'Shalom Aleichem.'"

"What is your memory of it?" I ask.

"I'm not sure, but I vaguely remember that it refers to angels."

"You're right," I reply. "That song actually welcomes the special Sabbath angels."

"Does that include Uriel?"

"I believe he is with you every day and night, whether or not it is the Sabbath."

"Maybe he is. I don't know. I've been feeling a little more relaxed. Maybe that's even been reflected in my dreams. Last night, the image of that picture on the wall appeared to me again."

"Which one?"

"The ship on the ocean. Except this time the sea was calm and the ship wasn't bobbing around as much."

"That's interesting," I reply. "Was anything else different?"

"Well, my feelings have changed, I think."

"In what way?"

"I used to think that the ship at the dock was safe and the one out to sea faced danger. But my perspective has changed a little. If *there's a bad storm, the one at the dock will be destroyed, too. And in the meantime, it hasn't gone anywhere."*

"That's a beautiful observation, Jonathan."

"Thank you. I think I'm less afraid of being on the ship that's moving. What do you think that means?"

"I think you already know, Jonathan. I think you are more comfortable with your soul – being on your own ship as it moves along its journey."

"I hope that's so. Maybe that's why some old line of poetry is going through my mind."

"Which one?" I ask.

"I don't know where it's from. All I know is that it came to me when I was thinking about the captain in the picture. In my dream, I still couldn't see his face. But after I woke up this morning, a recurring thought came to me. It was the phrase 'I am the master of my fate, I am the captain of my soul.' I think it's from a poem. Do you know who wrote it?"

"I can't remember right now. I'll have to look it up. But what do you think it means?"

"Maybe that I've got more control over my life than I thought. I can't do anything about the big issues, like when I will die. But I can control how I approach everything in life, including death."

"I think that is a very profound insight," I reply.

"Maybe Uriel has been communicating with me again," he says with a slight smile. "In any event, I've been doing more while I'm lying here. I've even spent some time listening to the classical music station when I feel up to it. Some of it actually gives me pleasure. I like slow, melodic pieces. Piano sonatas and nocturnes, things like that. But the music also stirs up a lot of feelings."

"Like what?" I ask.

"Well, I was listening to 'Four Seasons' by Vivaldi. It's beautiful

music, but it makes me sad. I look out and see the withered trees and I realize that it's almost winter. The other seasons will come and go, but I don't know how many more of them I'll see."

"That is very hard to think about. It's difficult to imagine a world without ourselves. How do you visualize the seasons that lie ahead?"

"I imagine they'll be like the ones I've already seen. Here in California, there aren't such huge differences from one time of year to another. There's lots of rain in the winter. Then we'll get some cooler weather until the springtime. It always gets cool and cloudy again in May and June before the summer begins. And then it's a long summer. Sometimes even in the fall we get heat waves. This really is a strange place."

"What part of the year do you like best?"

"I guess it's the springtime. I like the heat, but not when it's too intense. And I guess I like all the flowers and plants. I've got a beautiful jacaranda tree in my backyard and it blooms with purple blossoms every spring. I wonder if I'll get to see them again."

"What do you think of when you see the blossoms?"

"I guess it's sort of a cliche, but it makes me think of how things go in cycles."

"Can you elaborate?" I ask with a smile. We both laugh.

"If you mean that something that looks dead can come alive again, I guess that's what makes me feel happy and have hope. Look, I know what you're driving at. It's one thing, though, when we talk about flowers. I have to tell you, I've got a lot of trouble with that idea when it comes to people. Especially when it comes to me."

"I can understand that. I think that's true for most of us."

"Are you allowed to say that? Are you sure you're a Rabbi?"
We both smile.

"Seriously," he continues. "I don't want to make you feel bad,

but I still have a lot of trouble believing, especially about stuff I can't see."

"That doesn't make me feel bad at all. I respect your honesty. And as I've already told you, I have to struggle with all of these issues myself."

"When all is said and done, it still comes back to what I told you at the beginning. Everything still seems absurd to me in the face of death. Nothing seems worthwhile. I don't know how I can make peace with that."

"I think that is one of the major struggles of our life. Finding peace within, especially when it comes to things that are unknowable and unseeable."

"How can anyone ever come to terms with death? If we focus on it all the time, it's impossible to live during the time we've got. I don't know how we can ever make peace with death."

Chapter 34

MAKING PEACE WITH DEATH

EACH OF US can spend a lifetime trying to make peace with our mortality. Treating death in this way can remind us how to enjoy life. We can let the reality of death serve as a constant, gentle reminder about what is truly significant and what is inconsequential.

Some people are able to live in harmony with the valley of the shadow of death. One of them is an extraordinary young woman named Betsy, who underwent open heart surgery some years ago. Following her operation, Betsy had a near-death experience before she eventually recovered. While the staff worked to resuscitate her, Betsy encountered something wonderfully comforting; a complete acceptance of death based on her discovery of a place of calm, serenity and peace. And now, for the rest of her life, she will focus on what is truly important to her – love and the ability to make people laugh and enjoy life.

Not everyone will have a near-death experience, but we can all learn from those who have traveled to that place and returned. Death gently reminds us that life is not a rehearsal.

"I agree with you. But there's still the ultimate question of what becomes of us. We've often talked about the soul, which you believe is the eternal part of us. But it's such a foreign concept to my way of thinking. Seriously, how do you understand the soul?"

Chapter 35

THE SOUL

THE SOUL is elusive and almost impossible to describe. Perhaps it is not so surprising that in many languages, including Greek, Latin and Hebrew, the word for soul is identical with the word for breath. For example, in Greek, *psyche* refers to breath and soul. In Latin, *anima* is used for both. In Hebrew, the words for "*to breathe*" and "*soul*" share the same root, *n-sh-m*.

Breathing is the most constant, continuous aspect of our lives. It is crucial to our being alive. How we breathe is linked closely to our well-being. Some people meditate while focusing on each breath. This is a useful way to relax and center the mind and spirit. Even in the midst of excruciating pain, breathing exercises can actually bring a sense of temporary reprieve and relief.

One of the bravest people I have ever met is a young woman named Catherine, who has undergone a series of painful surgeries and medical procedures for congenital abnormalities. Catherine makes me wonder how I would deal with some of the challenges facing the patients and clients I meet. Her courage absolutely astounds me.

As I entered Catherine's room one day, I realized I could barely see her small, frail body on the bed in the midst of all the monitors, intravenous poles, tubes, catheters and other massive, noisy pieces of equipment clustered around her. I was surprised to see her looking so serene that at first I thought she was sleeping. Soon, however, she opened her eyes and spoke to me in a soft, weak voice.

"I'm glad you came to see me. I was just meditating. It's the only way I can get through the pain and make it through the day. I've learned how to focus on each breath that I take, in and out, and it's really something. I know I need the drugs too, but my breathing exercises help me feel more in control. Every time I feel a severe spasm of pain, I picture myself at the beach, watching the water, with a wave reaching a crescendo and then receding. When I breathe through that imagery, I feel the pain lessening."

The way we breathe reflects the state of our soul at any given moment. Our breaths may be quick and anxious or long and relaxed. Ultimately, however, the final breath, the final exhalation, is retrieved by God. Pain is then eliminated from our lives forever as our soul continues.

It is hard to grasp an elusive concept like the soul. For me, it is easiest to think of it as the Divine spirit of life or the eternal dimension of humanity.

Many years ago, I became friends with a prominent surgeon who was struggling with belief in God. One time he said to me, caustically and sarcastically, "You know, I've done surgery for a long time. I've seen every part of the body: spleen, liver, kidneys, intestines, ovaries – you name it. But there's one thing I've never seen and that's the soul. Where is it?"

"Are you married?" I asked him, "Yes," he replied, "to a lovely lady. We've been married for 12 years and have two kids."

"So, tell me, in all your explorations of the body, have you ever seen love?"

"No," he replied.

"But you've experienced it, right?" I continued.

"Definitely," he replied. "I certainly have."

Many physicians seem unable to understand that there is more to the world than what we can see through the naked eye or with a microscope or telescope. The 72-year-old wife of a prominent internist took me aside once at a hospital reception and told me she had something important to tell me.

"I know this isn't the time or the place, but I just have to go on record with my request to you. I don't know how much time I've got left. None of us ever does, but I've had a condition for quite a while and I don't know where things are heading. Anyhow, when the time comes, I want you to be there with me. I love my husband very much, as you know, but there are some things I just can't talk about with him. We can never discuss belief, the soul or things like that. He's a very rational guy, a scientist and he doesn't believe in any of this. But I've always felt sure that there is something beyond myself and I need someone who understands that. I want you to be with me when I'm ready to go."

I understood what this sincere woman was telling me, and I invited her to drop by my office from time to time so that we could discuss some of these issues without waiting for a crisis to occur.

This woman has discovered a truth that I hope she can convey to her husband. Neither the soul nor love can be seen, but we cannot live without either.

This woman's need to relate in a soulful manner is not unique. I meet many people like her husband in the course of my work. To them I quote:

There are more things in heaven and earth, Horatio,
Than are dreamt of in your philosophy.
– William Shakespeare, *Hamlet, I, v, 166*

"By the way, Jonathan, I see that we both share a love of poetic

words and images. I looked up that line you told me about: 'I am the master of my fate, I am the captain of my soul.' I found it in Bartlett's. A man named William Ernest Henley wrote it. He lived from 1849-1903."

"He didn't live for very long."

"You're right. But he left works that continue to speak to us, as you see."

Jonathan remains quiet, thinking. Then he speaks: "When I hear about the death of anyone else, even of someone who died almost a hundred years ago, I can't help thinking about my own mortality. Some things are very hard to fathom."

Jonathan is quiet again for a time. "May I ask you a favor, Rabbi?"

"Of course," I respond.

"Do you think you could get me a print of that picture on the wall. It's obviously had an impact on me if I'm dreaming about it. And I like it. It's beautiful."

"I'll certainly try," I respond. "I'll ask the hospital's Art Council if they can get a print for us."

"Thank you. I think it will help me, especially when I'm feeling down. There is something comforting about it. I like to look at it when my feelings overwhelm me. I find myself thinking a lot about the big questions, about what it is to be human. Even if we acknowledge a soulful life, we are still such limited physical beings. We exist in a frail body."

Chapter 36
THE BODY

THE BODY is the garment of the soul. The more the soul radiates, the more the body and face shine. The soul illuminates its environment.

We come into this world naked and we die naked and there need be no shame or embarrassment at birth or at death. The main difference between the hour of birth and the time of death is what we have done with our soul throughout our lifetime.

When a baby is born, he or she cries and everyone else smiles. A person may die with a smile on his or her lips, while other people cry. They are sad and bereft, while the one who has died is at peace. A woman recently asked me to reassure her that her husband was no longer in pain. I told her what I honestly believe, "We are suffering. He is not."

It is important to take care of the body during our lifetime, by exercising or joining a health club or doing whatever else is necessary to stay in shape. But it is also necessary to join "spiritual health clubs" in order to make the soul shine through the body.

Dr. James Kirsch once told me something that his late wife, Hilde, had said. Noting the enormous sums that women spend on makeup, she commented: "If you are in successful psychoanalysis, you will always look pretty." I agree with her.

"That's very sweet. But look what's happening to my body. You must have noticed how I'm getting thinner and thinner. I get scared when I catch a glimpse of my face in the mirror. Look how gaunt and drawn I've become. I certainly don't look very 'pretty.'"

"I think that depends on how we define the term. Have you noticed anything else happening over the course of our talks? Have there been any other changes in you?"

He pauses for a few minutes, thinking of our conversations. "Well, maybe I have become a little more open. I've shared some things with you that I've never shared with anyone and that surprises me. And you've got me talking about angels and souls, a lot of stuff I've never truly considered before."

"So what do you think is happening to you, Jonathan?"

"Maybe I'm looking deeper into myself."

"And what has made that possible?"

"I guess I don't have all my old defenses. I'm not quite on guard as much as I used to be. I let some new ideas penetrate."

"Do you think that might be because your skin is thinner now than it used to be?"

"What do you mean by that?"

"Well, you've talked about growing thinner as a kind of loss. Is it possible that there's another side to it, that you've actually gained something in the process?"

"You mean like letting some new ideas in?"

"I think so. I think that is a real possibility."

He is silent for a while, thinking about what we have just said. Then he speaks: "But I still have a problem with my body. It's frightening for me not to be in control of what's happening to it."

"Have there been any other times when you felt that way about your body?"

He is silent, thinking. Then, he says, with a smile: "Well, if you mean sex, I guess there were times when I was afraid of how I would

163

do, how I'd perform. But I told you. Miriam and I had a great sex life for the three years we lived together. It was only after we got married that things went downhill."

"What do you think happened?"

He pauses again. "Let me be a little more honest with you. I'll tell you what Miriam told me. She said I didn't seem as interested in her as a person, that I sometimes treated her as if she only had a beautiful body. She also said that it wasn't just about us. She didn't want to surrender to being penetrated and being out of control. She actually used those words."

"But that didn't bother her before you got married?"

"It didn't seem to. I think it may have been that once she thought about herself in the roles of 'wife' and 'mother,' she seemed to change. I think it may also have been about having kids."

"Was she happy about becoming pregnant?"

"Yes. But she sometimes seemed to be on an emotional roller coaster. She even went for counseling during those years when the kids were little."

"Did it help her?"

"She felt it did. She learned a whole new way of talking about herself and about us. Sometimes it made sense, but sometimes I got turned off by the jargon. I couldn't stand the psychobabble."

"Can you give me an example?"

"Well, you know. Like 'self-fulfillment,' 'my needs,' etc. She told me that her therapist helped her realize she was infatuated with me when she first met me. We had dreams of a great future together. She saw herself as the wife of a brilliant scientist."

"And then what happened?"

"Once she became a mother, she saw herself – and our relationship – in a new way. She loved the kids but she felt she could not open up. She said she felt as if we were starting to live parallel

lives. She also said something that really got to me."

"What was that?"

"She said I was a very controlling person."

"Is that true?"

"I think I've always been the sort of person who needs to be in charge of things. One of the things that attracted me to science was the chance to precisely quantify and classify everything. It's very hard for me to surrender to the unknown. When I am in control, my free-floating anxiety is reduced."

"What about Miriam?"

"In a way, I think she's like me. She was never able to totally surrender, either. She told me she feared emotional intimacy. Her therapist told her that she was protecting her inner core."

"What else did she learn during her therapy?"

"Well, she only shared some of it with me, of course. I remember one afternoon in particular, when she shocked me with another one of her insights. It was on a Sunday and we were down near the beach, having a drink at an outdoor café. I don't remember how the conversation began, but I remember where it led. The word 'power' came up and she said that she was scared about her lack of power as a woman. She told me that many of the arguments she initiated were her way of gaining some power in our relationship."

"How did you react to what she told you?"

"With shock, I guess. I never really looked at things that way. I certainly never thought of her as a power-seeker, but maybe that did explain a lot of the unilateral decisions that she was fond of making."

"Did she share any other insights with you?"

"Yes. She told me that she always doubted that she'd be loved for who she really was, including all her frailties, vulnerabilities and insecurities. That was one of the reasons she was always keeping

part of herself back. You know, the more I think about this, it's almost funny. I think Miriam and I have probably got a lot more in common than we thought."

"What do you mean?"

"Even my colleagues have told me that I keep some emotional distance. I know that my level of comfort means keeping some space between myself and others."

"Do you love Miriam?"

He pauses again. "The only truthful answer is that I completely love her with half my soul. I think when we first were together, I was able to love her entirely. But time and time again, I was never able to completely trust her. I was too afraid to let go."

"And what are you afraid of now?"

"I guess now I have to surrender and trust to that which is unknown and to God. That's what makes me so afraid."

"I think that is very perceptive of you," I reply.

Jonathan is silent again. Then he says: "It's really strange. We have souls, yet we exist in bodies. And our bodies have needs, very real needs. I told you once before that my wife had withdrawn from me physically and psychically. It's not just sex that I want or need, though. It's even being hugged and embraced."

"That is natural and normal," I remind him. "Everyone needs that."

"What do people do when they're all alone?"

"Sometimes it's very hard for them," I respond. "I know a very sweet widow who told me that she couldn't stand to go through a single week without getting a hug. When her son brought her groceries every Sunday, she always asked him to give her a big hug. Fortunately, he understood."

Jonathan is silent again. Finally, he speaks. "I feel that way, too. Especially since I've been sick, I don't get enough touching."

I ask, "May I hug you, Jonathan?"

He nods his affirmative reply.

I sit near the head of the bed and put my arms around him. He hugs me back with greater strength than I would have thought possible. I feel tears in my eyes. When I loosen my embrace and pull back, I look at Jonathan's face. I see he is crying, too. The power of touch has moved both of us.

Chapter 37

TOUCHING

TOUCHING IS ESSENTIAL throughout our lives. It is the first way a mother communicates with her infant, and as such, is vital to the bonding process. Babies who are not touched enough fail to thrive and develop normally.

Touching is certainly important in married life, as a couple gets to know one another intellectually, sexually and soulfully. Sexuality is an important part of life and there is a relationship between sexuality and mortality. They are both peak sensual experiences. At the height of sexual intimacy, one of the partners may even feel "ready to die." This reality is reflected in the French use of the phrase *petite mort,* meaning "little death," for the experience of orgasm.

However, while death is experienced alone, sexuality is the most intense form of togetherness. During the sexual act, two bodies become one as at no other time. It is this process that can give birth to new life.

Just as we are not in control at the moment of our death, we are not in control at the height of sexual passion. For many people, that inability to be in control evokes fear. However, when we let go of our need to be in psychic and physical control, the union is intensified in its oneness.

At the end of life, many patients yearn to be touched and held. As dying people give birth to their eternal selves, touching once again becomes an essential part of their birthing process. Frequently they are all alone, their spouses having already died. The gentle touch of caring, compassionate family, friends and caregivers often helps this birthing process proceed comfortably and lovingly.

A compassionate nurse named Linda is particularly sensitive to the need for touch in our lives. For several years, she has been working the night shift, from 11:00 p.m. to 7:00 a.m., in the oncology unit. Many patients are there for prolonged periods of time and she forges deep relationships with them and their families.

Some months ago, she became very close to Harry, who was in the final stages of his illness. Harry was 78. His wife had died years earlier and his two sons, busy with their own families, had limited time to spend with him. Even when they did visit, regions of their heart were elsewhere. Harry found it hard to tell them about his real feelings and needs. Late at night, when it was quiet on the unit, he found a good listener in Linda. She always seemed to be there when he needed to talk or even to cry. He trusted her and she helped alleviate some of his fear, as well as his pain.

Harry felt no shame in asking Linda to hold his hand for a few minutes at a time and Linda was always willing to be there for him. One night, he seemed reluctant to let her go and Linda promised that she would return later in her shift. She had learned from experience never to postpone a visit until the following day.

Even though Linda was busy with other duties on the unit, she made it a point to look in on Harry from time to time. At 6:00 a.m., he appeared to be sleeping, but Linda decided to go into his room anyhow. She had a strong feeling that it was important to be with him at that moment. As she stood quietly by his bedside, Harry opened his eyes and smiled at her. He motioned for her to sit down next to him and she complied. They held hands for a long time. When Linda finally rose to go, she bent over to give Harry a hug and kiss his forehead. "I never did that before, and I don't know why, but I felt I just had to do it," she later told me. She also stopped by Harry's room to wave goodbye to him when she went off duty at 7:00 a.m.

When Linda arrived for work the following evening, she learned that Harry had passed away earlier that day. She took comfort in knowing she had extended a final loving touch to this unique individual, who now rested in a Divine embrace.

"That's a beautiful image, one that I hope I can hang onto. But I'm not ready for that yet."

"I understand," I reply. "I've brought you something else to hang onto, Jonathan. I've got a surprise for you. The Art Council gave me a copy of your favorite picture. I've brought it up with me."

Jonathan's face lights up. He reminds me of a child who is opening a birthday present. "Thank you, thank you," he says softly. "I will treasure this."

"You're welcome. I'm glad we could get it for you."

Several minutes pass in silence. Then Jonathan continues: "I'm deeply touched by your caring. However, I still need more than words and caring. Maybe I'm still looking for love, just as I have been for most of my life."

Chapter 38

LOVE

LOVE REALLY DOES make the world go 'round. And there are many kinds of love. What we need most throughout life and in the dying process is spiritual love.

When most people think of love, they associate it with physical intimacy, sex and sensuality. These are all important, of course, but there is another, deeper form of relationship that involves connecting with the mind, the soul and the heart of another. It is a form of complete acceptance and pure trust. It has no hidden agenda.

One retired physician expressed this thought to me when he described his relationship with his wife, which was now stronger than ever. "Things are so much better now," he said. "My gonads are not so active and they're not such a distraction anymore." What he was describing so well, was that hormonal changes that accompany aging can bring about very positive changes in a relationship. While they may cause a diminished desire for sexual love, they can increase the spiritual love between the two partners. My colleague went on to tell me of the shared visions, values, reminiscences and hopes that play an increasingly important role in his marriage.

One elderly grandmother told me that at this stage of her life, all she wants from her friends and family is love. By this, she means those small everyday acts that demonstrate caring and compassion, shared experiences that help create even deeper bonds.

When we feel most lonely and vulnerable, the presence of those people with whom we share spiritual love can comfort us. What is remarkable is that even *thinking* about such people can drive away our loneliness. Just imagining their healing presence, envisioning their faces and *hearing* their words can uplift us.

Cindy, a 38-year-old with metastatic cancer, told me how a childhood friend helped her from 3,000 miles away. "Lucy is my best friend in the whole world," she told me. "We've known each other since the seventh grade and we lived near each other all through college. I always call her 'Bunny' and she calls me 'Happy Face.' I can't even remember when that began, but it's been going on forever. We've always been able to talk about anything together, stuff we don't even share with our husbands because they don't talk about feelings and ideas the way we do. Bunny and I have kept in touch all these years. It's good that phone rates are so cheap because we talk so often. We know each other so well that we can almost finish each other's sentences.

"All through this illness, Bunny has been calling almost every day and sends me funny cards and notes. We e-mail each other when I feel up to it. Last time I was in the hospital, she sent me a big bunch of balloons. One had a big smiley face on it and the card said, 'A happy face for Happy Face.' I know it sounds corny, but it did make me smile. For a moment, we were back in school together, without a care in the world. She really loves me and I never have to worry about anything that we say to each other."

Such total acceptance is the key to spiritual love. This is particularly true for a dying person. There is no "right" way or "wrong" way to die. Accept the person as he or she is and the way that he or she wants to die.

Love people as they genuinely are. This acceptance will bring healing to your life, their lives and to the world.

"So is it as simple as that? Is our mission in life just to love each other?"

"The life mission for every person is as unique as that person. Most people have some internal feeling of what their purpose in life may be, although they do not usually put those feelings into words. And yes, for many, loving others in a genuine way is the highest form of self-fulfillment."

Chapter 39

LIFE'S MISSION

DR. ERWIN ALTMAN and Dr. Manfred Altman shared their depth of spiritual understanding with me before their deaths. Erwin Altman described his life mission this way[7]:

> Man's aim in the here-and-now is centered in his realization that he is responsible for his part in this continuum, both as giver and recipient of love. This leads to walking in the Divine path in daily life, to true self-realization by the love of one's self and of all fellow-men and all creations, to inspirational and uplifting love and joy of life, honest search for truth in all spheres, the search for creative expansion of one's unique potentialities, to the service of God through prayer, contemplation and above all, through the service to mankind and the universe, by the spirituality of thought, word, and action.

In the summer of 1999, just days before he passed away in London, Manfred and I spoke about many of the issues that we had discussed over the years. In elaborating on his life motto *"And Be A*

---

[7] *Ibid.*, p. 126.

Blessing" (Genesis 12:2), Manfred shared some of his thoughts with me. He understood life's mission as "to add to the goodness of the human potential, thereby adding to the glory of God and diminishing suffering."

We can do this through example and action. By looking for the positive and for opportunities to perform positive acts, we can affect change in the world.

Manfred was an original thinker who spent years reading, formulating and acting on his philosophy of life. But formulating an individual mission is something within reach of each of us. Our goal does not need to be profound or scholarly.

John, who was visiting Los Angeles from his home in New York, told me about something he did which gave him great pleasure and satisfaction. "Every day, I drive into Manhattan," he said, "and as you can imagine, I have to put up with a lot of traffic and other stress. One dreary Monday, I was having a really bad day, which I thought was a pretty rotten way to start the week. While I was waiting in line to pay the toll on the New Jersey Turnpike, I suddenly thought about that bumper-sticker idea of doing a random act of kindness. And you know what I did? I told the woman in the toll booth that I wanted to pay for the car in back of me, as well as for myself. I can't tell you what satisfaction it gave me to look in the rearview mirror and see the expression on that driver's face when he got up to the booth. He couldn't believe that someone had given him a little gift on a rainy Monday. I might have an over-active imagination, but I like to think that maybe he was a bit nicer than usual to the next person he met, and so on and so on and so on."

Even simple gestures can make a big difference in our lives and we can formulate them into something even greater than that. We all know that corporations have formal mission statements, which they revise periodically. However, *each* of us can work on our own, unique mission statement, printed or not. This can guide us throughout our lives, as well as help us prepare for our final journey. Instead of writing your epitaph, try to write your own mission statement.

"Is that what I'm supposed to leave behind? A copy of my will and my mission statement?"

"You will leave much more than that, I promise you. But I have another suggestion. In addition to thinking about a formal mission statement of your life goals, you might want to consider composing an ethical will for your children."

"An ethical will? I've never heard of such a thing."

Chapter 40

ETHICAL WILLS

WRITING A MISSION statement for our life is similar to composing an ethical will. Such a document describes the ethical and moral guidelines that we have lived by and that we wish to transmit to our children.

When we leave this world, we take none of our possessions with us. They are all left behind, to be distributed among our heirs, the state or strangers. Our values and our ethics are what will truly endure.

Unfortunately, no document can ever ensure that our values or our name will be transmitted to future generations. One man actually came into my office with a beautiful, handwritten ethical will that had been passed down from his grandfather, to his father and finally to him. Although he had preserved this lovely piece of calligraphy, he confided to me that he had not lived completely in accordance with all the principles it outlined.

"My grandfather was a very conservative man," said Joe. "He believed in doing things the old-fashioned way, living modestly within your means, always saving for the future and not going into debt. But times have changed. I've had to pay for a lot of things in a hurry and the only way I could do it was to run up the tab on my credit card. In the past year or so, things have really gotten out of hand and I'm afraid I might even have to declare bankruptcy. I can only imagine what Grandpa Lou would say about that!"

As this story shows, there is no foolproof way to ensure that our values will be transmitted to those who come after us. But the best way to try to achieve that goal is by *living those values*, so that our actions reflect our true beliefs. Children are quick to understand the real message that is being sent to them. They may be taught "Honor Thy Father and Thy Mother" in religious school, but they will more likely care for a parent as they witnessed that parent care for his or her own mother and father.

The way we approach death becomes a crucial part of our ethical will, written or unwritten. By our words and actions, we demonstrate to our children not only how to die, but also how to live.

"I hope I've given something of value to my kids. But there's a lot more that I've got to talk to them about and I don't know if I'll have time."

"None of us knows how much time we have. That is why we need to make the most of each moment."

"But it's hard to focus on stuff beyond myself right now. My pain and my survival needs are the focus of my life at this point."

"I understand and respect that. What you say is true."

"So how can I focus on these spiritual things when my body has so many needs? I already told you, it's not even just the pain. I also need to be loved."

"That's true. As long as we occupy physical bodies, we continue to have those needs. They are central to our being."

"And then a time will come when I won't exist in this body any more?"

"That's right. You will continue as a completely spiritual being."

"It's very hard to accept that separation."

"That's true. It is hard for all of us."

"What can you say to make it easier?" he asks.

"Let me make a suggestion," I reply. "Close your eyes and meditate for as long as you like, the way that we have been practicing together. See what thoughts come to you. Perhaps Uriel will visit you again."

Jonathan reaches for my hand and I take it. He closes his eyes and begins breathing deeply. He remains that way for close to 10 minutes, not moving or saying anything. At last, he opens his eyes and I see that they are filled with tears.

"I don't know if it was Uriel speaking to me or not, but I did get some sort of insight. Maybe it was from him."

"Would you like to share it with me?"

"It was just something about this whole process. Worrying about the future. Worrying about my body. I'm struggling so much with my body as I'm also preparing to leave it. I'm getting ready for the transition to the next level of experience. I am getting ready to pass my torch to those who will follow me."

First Heaven

Lighting Your Own Candle

Life on Earth

Second Heaven

Gathering the Sparks

The Present is Part of Eternity

Third Heaven

Sheltering the Flame

Protecting Your True Inner Voice

Fourth Heaven

Brightening the Flame

Accepting Being Human

Fifth Heaven

Illuminating the Way

Angels on Earth

Sixth Heaven

Lighting the Next Candle

Passing the Torch

Part VII

BECOMING ONE WITH THE LIGHT

PROLOGUE

IT IS SATURDAY afternoon at 5:00 p.m. It is the Jewish Sabbath and I have walked a short distance from my home to the hospital.

I knock and enter Jonathan's room. The curtains have been drawn back to allow as much light as possible to enter. The whole room is illuminated by the rays of the sun which will soon be setting.

Jonathan's head is propped up on two pillows and he is gazing out the window.

"Hello, Jonathan. How are you doing today?" I ask.

He turns toward me and smiles. "They tell me I'm actually doing better, for now. But I know how it is. I get better, then I get worse. I don't think they're even going to let me stay in the hospital much longer. You know, it all boils down to insurance coverage."

We both smile. "So where will you go next?" I ask.

"That's a good question. I'm not sure. I could go home, but Miriam can't take care of me by herself. We could have aides around the clock, but it's a huge expense and they wouldn't be registered nurses, which is what I really need."

"What are some of your other options?"

"Well, I could go to a rehabilitation hospital and stay there for a while, as long as I continue to make some progress. There is also

2

another choice that I have to consider."

"What's that?"

"Well, my health insurance offers care at a hospice facility. It's supposed to be clean and well-run. I've seen pictures of it. It has a nice garden."

"How do you feel about it?"

"I don't think I'm ready to go there yet. It seems to me that it might as well have a sign on the door, saying 'Abandon hope, all ye who enter here.' If I go there, I know I'll be buying a one-way ticket."

"Is anyone pressuring you to make such a decision?"

"No. Not really. I think Miriam and the kids want me to go to the rehab place for a while. That way, we can all pretend that I've got more time than I have."

"Do you want to go on pretending?"

He pauses. "No. Not really. I've been thinking about some of the things we've discussed. I also saw a tape that had a good effect on me."

"Which one was that?" I ask.

"It showed a big gathering of cancer survivors. They were having a day of celebration. The whole works – balloons, refreshments and speeches. One person really made an impression on me."

"Who was that?"

"A young woman, about 23 at the most. She had short dark hair. I think it's just growing back after her chemotherapy treatments. She's got a terrific spirit."

"Tell me about her."

"Well, she had a freak case of breast cancer at that unbelievably early age. It was pretty aggressive. She lives in London but she came here for treatment. Most of the doctors gave her a poor prognosis. One doctor thought that a stem cell transplant might offer her a chance, but it had never been successful with her type of cancer."

"What happened?"

"This one doctor believed that the transplant was worth a try, though the procedure almost destroys you even when it works. He persuaded the other doctors to give her a shot at it. And she made it. Now she wants to go into medicine or nursing and help others."

"Did she talk about her experiences as a patient?"

"Yes. She shared some stories that I could sure identify with. The way that other people treat you. The procedures you go through. But more than that, it was her spirit that touched me. At the end of her remarks, she – ", Jonathan's *voice breaks and tears fill his eyes. He composes himself and continues:"She sang. She has a beautiful voice. She sang, 'The Impossible Dream.'" Tears stream down his face as he continues: "It was the most beautiful thing I have ever heard. Not just the words and the melody, but what it meant that she was here to sing them. I think she gave a lot of people hope."*

"Did she give you hope, too?"

"I think so. I connected with her. Maybe another kind of hope. I told you that I was impressed with her spirit. That reminds me of a discussion we've had before. When I say 'spirit,' I'm acknowledging something you can't see but you know is there. Maybe I'm ready to accept that possibility."

"I'm pleased to hear that. Was there anything else in the program that was particularly meaningful?"

"There were a lot of good moments. One speaker said that hope was one of the most important tools in the doctor's bag and I guess I agree with that. I also thought of something that I read in your book 'Ancient Secrets.' [8]*"*

"What was that?"

"You said that even when a cure is not possible, healing is

---

[8] Meier, L. *Ancient Secrets: Using the Stories of the Bible to Improve Our Everyday Lives.* Woodstock, Vermont: Jewish Lights, 1999, p. 187.

always possible. Do you believe that?"

"Yes," I reply. "Do you?"

"Maybe. I've been looking at things in a new way. I'm allowing myself to think about things I never considered before."

"That's good," I reply. "You're still growing."

"I guess I am. I don't think I'm as angry as I was at first. You know what used to go through my mind? Something that Dylan Thomas wrote: 'Rage, rage against the dying of the light.' Well, that's how I felt."

"And now?"

"I'm not sure, but for whatever reason, I don't feel quite so angry any more. Maybe I'm a little more at peace with myself."

"That's good. You're a very special man, Jonathan. You have a brilliant mind and a beautiful soul. I really enjoy your sharing your thoughts and observations with me. Your name is an apt description of who you are."

"What do you mean?"

"In Hebrew, Jonathan means a gift from God and you are a gift to me."

His eyes well with tears once again. "Thank you, Rabbi. Thank you for telling me that. I feel we can really speak on a deep level. I'm sorry I've never been able to do that with anyone else."

"There is still time," I remind him.

"You're right," he says. "There is. But I'm still not sure how to talk about the things that really matter with the people who are closest to me – my family. Why is it harder with my family than with anyone else?"

Chapter 41
FAMILY

FAMILIES SHOULD COME with warning labels. They are not always good for our health. Family members can be very supportive or they can make a dying person very uncomfortable. What matters most is whether a family can transcend personal concerns and serve as a positive catalyst during a dying person's final journey.

My experience has taught me that family conflicts will most likely become exacerbated at times of crisis. However, despite any negative past experiences, a dying person may still want family to be around.

Family dynamics may certainly continue to change throughout the dying process and after. The death of someone, particularly a family patriarch or matriarch, affects everyone in the family. Family bonds may become stronger or may weaken. The death of someone close often makes us think of our own mortality and that affects all of our relationships.

It is impossible to speak about families as though there were one simple truth that can be applied to all of them. When I was young, the definition of "family" seemed fairly simple. It meant two parents and their children living in the same household. Certainly, that is no longer the norm. The vast majority of families with whom I have contact are not simple nuclear structures. They are sometimes headed by one parent. They often include children from more than one marriage or relationship. They sometimes include a grandparent and occasionally the grandparent is the one actually rearing the children.

Even when we see what appears to be a "perfect" family, that is rarely the case. I think of my friend Carl, who is fond of telling about a Thanksgiving dinner he attended some years ago in the Midwest.

"I hadn't been back to Iowa in a long time," he confided. "For me, it was like time travel. All those picturesque farms and homes. It seems as if nothing ever changes there. And when I sat down to dinner at my friend's home, I felt as if I'd stepped into a Norman Rockwell painting – the whole family sitting around the table, with the turkey, the yams, the whole bit. I should have taken a picture.

"Then, right before dessert, I felt a headache coming on," Carl continued. "I excused myself and went to the bathroom. I'm really not a snoop and all I wanted was an aspirin, but when I opened the medicine cabinet, I was in for a big surprise. I saw two types of anti-anxiety medicines and an anti-depressant drug on the second shelf. There's nothing wrong with that, of course, but it was just such a surprise. I was with people who acted as if they didn't have a care in the world."

Family dynamics are particularly delicate during milestone events. I know of one case where what happened in the days and hours preceding a death nearly destroyed a family.

Sidney was nearly 69 years old and dying of lung cancer. His wife of 40 years, Lorraine, was very attentive to him throughout his illness. During the last months of his life, he was constantly in and out of the hospital. Even when he slept at home, he regularly came to the hospital's outpatient cancer center for chemotherapy and radiation treatments.

During what proved to be Sidney's last hospitalization, shortly before his birthday, Sidney and Lorraine both realized he didn't have much time left. As a final loving gesture, Lorraine decided to throw a birthday party for him right there in his hospital room. It would be a final celebration of his life for family and close friends.

Lorraine brought telephone lists from home to her husband's room. She began going through the names to get his approval for the invitations. Lorraine reached the name of a woman, "Roberta," whom they had known for years, someone whom they occasionally saw socially, but more often through business functions or at their club.

Lorraine assumed that upon hearing Roberta's name, Sidney would quickly respond "No." But surprisingly, he gave an immediate, enthusiastic "Yes." When she asked him to explain, he waved his hand, saying, "It's my dying wish. That's all you need to know. She's got to be there."

Lorraine began to wonder if there was more to this relationship than she knew. She thought back to occasional nights when her husband worked late and told her not to even try to call him, since it would be disruptive. She'd always thought of Roberta as being rather aloof, but noted her polish and grace, qualities she felt she herself lacked. It was not possible, but could there be something between Sidney and Roberta? Surely that was completely out of the question.

But as Sidney approached the end of his life, he found the need to say things, admit things and share things that he had never told her before. Yes, he confirmed, he had had more than a casual relationship with Roberta. Yes, it had been going on for quite a while. No, he would not reconsider. Yes, he absolutely wanted Roberta to come to his birthday party.

Lorraine was understandably stunned and confused. Could she refuse her husband's deathbed request? But what about her own feelings? Didn't she have any say in the matter? Where was Sidney's love and regard for her – which he still proclaimed? Lorraine was

190

even more hurt when she discovered that her own children had known and covered up this extramarital romance. They wanted to be loyal to their father who had always been loving and generous towards them, and they felt that Roberta made their father happy.

It is impossible to know what motivated Sidney to bare his soul at that moment. It may have been an act of hostility, an attempt to punish Lorraine for some past wrong, real or imagined. There can be a multitude of reasons for truth-telling, which is clearly not always a good thing.

Lorraine and Sidney called me to his hospital room and asked me what to do. Without knowing all of the factors and given the immediacy of the party, I tried to come up with some sort of solution that would suit both of them. I'm not sure I succeeded, but after I talked with both of them, they suggested that Roberta come very late to the party. By that time, Lorraine and most of the other guests would have left. Then, Sidney, his children and Roberta would have some time together. That suggestion seemed acceptable to everyone concerned.

I do not claim that it was Solomonic or wise or even right. At times, I realize that even in the face of death, things cannot always be wrapped up neatly. Often there are no clear-cut solutions. No one answer is right for everyone.

"I agree with you there, Rabbi. I can't imagine how that family ever got through that ordeal. I don't know how Lorraine and Sidney managed to stay together so long. I don't know how Miriam and I have made it this far either."

"Jonathan, sometimes no complete resolution with one's immediate family is possible. However, we can find strength in recognizing that we are not only part of a family and a community, but also members of the human family. And we all share being fallible."

191

"That's a nice sentiment, but I don't feel that connected even to my own family, let alone to any other community. I'm not a joiner. Other people might belong to a church or a synagogue, but not me. I guess my work has been the closest thing to a religion for me and I don't see any of my colleagues anymore. So when you talk about being part of some collective, I'm not even sure what you really mean."

Chapter 42

BEING GATHERED TO YOUR PEOPLE

MOST PEOPLE think about death as a separation from those they love. But it can also be viewed as a process of gathering together with other loved ones.

When young people set out in life, most expect to find a soul mate to ease their aloneness. They envision a special sweetheart who will be at their side through times of joy and sorrow, and who will bring them companionship, comfort and consolation. However, the reality is that many people end up being alone together.

This sad truth was expressed to me a few years ago by one of my clients, Harriet. She told me that she was very excited about her approaching fortieth wedding anniversary. She was just starting to make plans for the event and she tried to involve her husband, Tim, in some of the decision-making. He responded, "What are we celebrating?"

Harriet was wounded to the core. She couldn't believe her husband's words or tone. She asked him to meet with me and he agreed. During our very first session, it became clear that his view of his marriage differed sharply from that of his wife. "We don't have a real relationship," he told me. "We lead parallel lives."

Tim described a situation that is true for many, many people. How sad that individuals marry to escape aloneness, yet often encounter it in another form. How sad that we cannot become more comfortable with our aloneness and discover the richness of solitude. When we become comfortable with ourselves, we no longer need to seek an idealized soul mate in any one person. Instead, we recognize our intrinsic connectedness to *all other people*.

That realization is particularly important during the dying process. Even though a dying person is on his or her unique lonely journey, the Bible uses an interesting, comforting phrase describing death: *"And be gathered unto your people"* (Deuteronomy 32:50). This refers to your community, your ancestors and your descendants, even those not yet born.

We each live in a certain time period, but we are each also part of a much greater collective, one that stretches from the distant past to the distant future.

This collective includes our family, our extended family, our heritage, our culture, our country and indeed, the whole of humanity. Truly understanding life in this way will lessen our fear of death by letting us realize that we are never truly alone – in this reality or the next.

Ultimately, we are all one people who share this one planet. Although there are salient differences between us, we also have a lot in common. We all struggle with relationships on a daily basis. And in the end, we are all one.

"As a scientist, I certainly agree with what you are saying. There is no question that we are more alike than different. But, truthfully, you and I know that there are many cultural, religious and other differences between people. Every group and sub-group has its own practices and customs. Don't we all pray differently?"

"That may be true in some sense. But I think the more fundamental issue is what is the essence of prayer."

"I'm not sure I follow. Isn't it always a prescribed religious text, along with some kneeling and bowing?"

"I can understand why you might think of prayer that way. Many people do. You're describing liturgical traditions. But I think of prayer in a different sense. Prayer takes place in a house of worship and wherever else you are. Furthermore, prayer can be both structured and spontaneous. Prayer at times is a monologue, but it can also reach a level where it is a dialogue."

Chapter 43
PRAYER

DIALOGUE BETWEEN MAN and God occurs through prayer, contemplation, meditation and feeling. Every living moment can be a prayer to God.

One patient thanked God for the gift of life even as he lay dying. One man prayed he would be as conscious as possible until his last breath so he could create positive thoughts for his transition from life to death. So, too, what we think and feel creates our experience of any event, including prayer.

Etty Hillesum created her own prayers under incredibly adverse conditions. She was a 29-year-old Dutch Jew who spent the last months of her life in Westerbork, a transit camp in the Netherlands for those being deported to Auschwitz. There, she nursed the sick in the hospital barracks and wrote in her diary about her spontaneous need for prayer[9]:

> "...Time and again it soars straight from my heart – I can't help it, that's just the way it is, like some elementary force – the feeling that life is glorious and magnificent..."

---

[9] Hillesum, Etty. (1985). *An Interrupted Life: The Diaries of Etty Hillesum,* 1941 - 43. New York: Pocket Books, p. 247.

In another entry, written several months before her death, she wrote[10]:

> You have made me so rich, oh God, please let me share Your beauty with open hands. My life has become an uninterrupted dialogue with You, oh, God, one great dialogue. Sometimes when I stand in some corner of the camp, my feet planted on Your earth, my eyes raised towards Your Heaven, tears sometimes run down my face, tears of deep emotion and gratitude. At night, too, when I lie in my bed and rest in You, oh, God, tears of gratitude run down my face, and that is my prayer...My life is one great dialogue with You.

Even as Hillesum was being deported to Auschwitz in 1943, knowing too well what awaited her and her people, she wrote a note on a postcard, expressing her joy at being able to sing. Her singing was a form of prayer.

Although there are almost no atheists in foxholes, not everyone knows how to pray or what to pray for when death approaches.

Throughout life, during moments of despair, many people pray, "I want to die," either aloud or quietly to themselves. But one of life's ironies is that when death finally approaches, most people say or pray, "I hope it's not my time yet. I want to live. When I said I wanted to die, I only meant for the pain to stop."

I recently recited the traditional final prayer with a woman who was in a special care unit for terminally ill patients. Afterwards she said, "I wish I could go home and bake one more cake for my grandson."

---

[10] Hillesum, Etty. (1986). *Letters From Westerbork*. New York: Pantheon Books, p. 116.

At such a holy moment, the priorities of life are clearer than ever before. *This* is the time to be with your children, grandchildren and friends, to empower them with your final spiritual legacy, one that will stay with them forever.

One patient taught me the following prayer:

Reach into your innermost self,
Into your quiet, peaceful center,
And open yourself up
To God, to love, to forgiveness.
Let go of everything – of anger,
Of pain,
Of self-pity,
Of all the things that bind you.

"You speak of communicating with God, but I can't even communicate with people properly. Soon I won't be able to communicate at all. I wonder if I'll regret the things I haven't said to my wife and kids, just as I regret the things I didn't say to my father and mother."

"What has made that so difficult for you?"

"A lot of things. Fear of the unknown and of revealing some deeper parts of myself. I'm afraid that what I share will not be adequately received or understood. I sometimes wonder if I've ever truly been able to express myself."

Chapter 44

COMMUNICATION

THROUGHOUT LIFE, we express ourselves through the written and spoken word. Most of us do not realize that there are other forms of communication as well, such as art and music, which are deep expressions of the self. Furthermore, the way we dress, our personal hygiene, the way we comb our hair, our mannerisms, our posture, and all of our personal choices also reflect aspects of ourselves that we communicate to others.

There is also unconscious communication. Our dreams, as bizarre as they may sometimes seem, are our psyche's way of communicating with us.

In the recesses of our very private thoughts, we also communicate with close friends and relatives who have died. Somehow these conversations give us a measure of comfort and a sense that each of us is a link in the chain of continuity from the beginning of the world through eternity.

The dead are not alive in the conventional sense. Yet, they have spiritual life and are always available to us, particularly when fears overtake us and we feel vulnerable, especially as we face our own death. That is why dying patients often talk to their deceased mother or father or both. Doing this gives them the strength to make the transition and rejoin their people.

Rabbi Levi Meier

"But I have a problem that continues to gnaw at me. I've told you that I've become more open to some ideas. But at the core of my being, I'm still not at all certain what I believe. I would like to believe the things you've told me. I would also like to believe that an angel called Uriel or some other being has been speaking to me through dreams or visions. But part of my brain still has tremendous trouble with those ideas. Part of me still cannot accept concepts that other people, like you, seem to accept without difficulty."

Chapter 45

FOR THOSE WHO DON'T BELIEVE

ALL OF US struggle with our beliefs. If we are honest with ourselves, we recognize that they evolve over a period of time and are continually being modified and refined. Our beliefs are certainly important to us throughout our lives and particularly as we contemplate our deaths. I recently visited a woman who was dying. She told me that she was afraid. When I asked what frightened her most, she replied, "Death, because I don't believe in anything afterwards."

Perhaps you are like her in some way. Perhaps you believe in life, but not in life after life. No matter what your doubts, no matter what your views, I respect your belief system. Your own values are unique. They might reflect your parents' teachings and actions, your culture and society, as well as your personal struggles and circumstances.

Some books offer extraordinary descriptions of people who have gone to the brink of death and returned. Invariably, their near-death experiences have given them a sense of hope, tranquility and peace. But I do not want to try to "prove" that there is life after life.

My own personal belief is that there are two types of life – when the body and soul are together and when the soul is by itself. Space and time are concepts that apply only to where the body is. The soul, however, returns to God. After death, there is a life of the soul, which is beyond our comprehension because our understanding of life is so essentially connected with space and time.

Throughout our lives, we all continue to change. Change is one of the hallmarks of healthy growth. Let me tell you about a woman who recently came to see me, expressing a desire for change in her life. Only 63 years old, she is dying of heart disease. She has been married for 40 years and has three grown children. In the course of our discussions, she confided numerous things to me: "You know, Rabbi, I didn't really marry for love. I just wanted security and Jack was able to give it to me. For that, I even married out of my faith. I gained wealth, social standing and prestige. Those seemed to be the most important things in life. Now I realize that I sold myself!" At this stage of her life, her focus is very different as she examines and reevaluates her life. She summarized her new goals saying, "I have lived a Godless life, but now I want to reconnect with God and with my people."

"I also want to reconnect with God and my people. Last year, I attended your High Holiday services. On Yom Kippur, they recited a prayer that bothered me a lot."

"Why was that?"

"It's something hard for me to talk about, but I trust you enough to share it." Jonathan is silent for a few moments, then continues: "One prayer talked about being inscribed in the Book of Life or the Book of Death during the coming year. I can't help thinking that I was inscribed in the Book of Death. After all, I'm likely to die before the next Yom Kippur."

I do not respond immediately. "I really appreciate your telling me about that, Jonathan. Yom Kippur must have been a very difficult time for you. You raise a really important question. It's one that I've also thought about a lot. Can I share my understanding with you?"

"Of course. I'd welcome it." I continue. "When someone dies, the body is buried and disintegrates in the earth. But the soul is retrieved by means of God's kiss, as we've already discussed. It returns to its Divine source. In a physical sense, death has occurred. But I see things from a broader perspective. I think that during this past Yom Kippur, you were inscribed in the Book of Life."

Jonathan is startled. He looks at me with questioning, hopeful eyes. "What do you mean by that?" he asks. "How can I die, yet be inscribed in the Book of Life?"

I reach forward and take his hand. "Remember that every moment of your life is part of eternal life, Jonathan. Even when you physically die, you will still continue your eternal life, but this time it will be on a purely spiritual level."

Jonathan grips my hand with greater strength. He looks more relaxed and appears comforted. "Is that what the prayer really conveys?" he asks.

"Yes," I reply. "I believe so. Those who have died are inscribed in the Book of Eternal Life. But something else can be learned from the image of the two books. I think that some people may be walking around who are not really alive."

Jonathan looks shocked. He says: "What do you mean by that?"

"I think that our definitions of life and death do not have to be so literal. For me, being alive means much more than the beating of a heart or the existence of brain waves. Being alive involves being engaged in life-affirming activities, being truly engaged in whatever you are doing."

"You mean like stopping to smell the roses?"

"Yes, but not just on an occasional basis. Life is having a sense of awe and wonder at the incredible beauty and complexity of the world around you. That's what I call living in the moment, as we've discussed before. Have you ever heard of a poem by William Blake

called 'Auguries of Innocence'?"

"I don't remember. It doesn't sound familiar."

"Let me share four lines from that work with you. I've quoted them so often that I know them by heart:

To see a World in a Grain of Sand,

And a Heaven in a Wild Flower,

Hold Infinity in the palm of your hand,

And Eternity in an hour.

Jonathan is silent for a few minutes. Then he says: "That's really nice. I like the way he puts it. So you're telling me that a sense of awe and wonder is the key to a meaningful life?"

"I think so. It also involves being a catalyst for others and helping them in their growth and development."

"Is that why you became a Rabbi and psychologist?"

"I have a passion for listening to the suffering voices of the soul because I also have an unfailing faith in the potential of each living soul."

Jonathan is silent for some time. Then he speaks. "I've never heard things explained that way before. Your words appeal to me. I know that you believe in me and that you love me. That is very precious."

"Thank you for telling me that, Jonathan. You have touched me deeply."

"I no longer feel that I have to hide any part of myself from you. I feel totally visible and revealed to you."

"I am honored, Jonathan. I have also shared things with you that I have never shared with anyone else."

He is quiet again. When he finally speaks, his voice is soft and I strain to hear him.

"I appreciate that very much. You've opened my eyes to some

new possibilities. You've helped me rediscover the power of wonder."

"How?"

"I realize that I've often taken my work on the human genome somewhat for granted. But when my granddaughter first heard the news reports about our discoveries, she said, 'That's totally amazing.' Maybe it's good to view the world through the eyes of a child."

"I agree with you," I reply.

Jonathan continues. 'So that's your view of life. What about death?"

"Well, as I told you, I believe there is bodily death. But there are other kinds of death as well."

"Such as?"

"What do you think I mean?" I ask.

"I suppose you mean people who aren't fully alive."

"That's right. And who are they?"

"I have some ideas, but I'd like to hear your opinion."

"There are many kinds of people who are technically alive, but don't appreciate the gift of life. They feel only a great emptiness, a tremendous void inside. They find no meaning in their existence. They are constantly critical and can't or won't appreciate the wonder around them. They wander aimlessly in depression and despair or are so embittered that they can never glimpse any light. Those people are not really alive at all."

"I've felt that way myself at times. When I've felt depressed, I experienced life as a living death. I once told my doctor something that we laughed about, but maybe it was a real Freudian slip."

"What was that?"

"I looked at the slides of my tumor and I wanted to say something about the cancer of the cell. But it didn't come out that

way. I ended up saying 'cancer of the soul.'"

"I think you have discovered a great truth," I reply.

Jonathan is quiet, then softly says, "I've never thought about these things before. Maybe learning to see things in a new way can help me – even now. I know there aren't any easy answers. But I'm hoping that our talks can at least give me some peace of soul."

"I hope so, too. Do you want to know how I understand peace of soul?"

"Yes, please."

"For me, it represents the final stage in our approach to death. Most of us are familiar with the five stages that were first described by Elizabeth Kubler-Ross: denial, anger, bargaining, depression and finally, acceptance. Yet there is another stage beyond acceptance, one that can truly liberate us as we approach the end of our physical lives. That stage is what I call peace of soul. It is a process as well as a way of being."

"How are we supposed to achieve inner peace?"

"I hope the thoughts and meditations we've shared have helped. In particular, I hope our discussions about learning to recognize the union of opposites in life can help. Death is a part of life, just as shadow is a part of light."

"Well, I hope our talks will help me find unity in my life. Until now, I've been the pure scientist and helped to map the human genome. But we've discussed a lot of spiritual and metaphysical matters. Don't you think we should undertake a project to map the human soul?" he asks with a smile.

"I think that's a great idea," I reply. "And you are the perfect person to do it."

"I've learned that although we can clone a cell, we can't clone a soul. Maybe that will be my legacy," he says quietly. "Who knows? Who would have thought I'd be feeling like this? Maybe my soul

work will help prepare me for my own death. Even saying that out loud – 'my own death' – is still hard for me. But I know that day is approaching – soon. My eyes will close for the last time and my doctor will record the time and fill out a death certificate for me. And he's going to put down a cause of death. In my case, it's cancer."

"That's true, Jonathan. But there's another cause as well. We don't really die from illness. Death is a natural sequel to life. On every death certificate, the cause of death should really be 'life.'"

"So more than anything else, you, my grandfather and Uriel are reminding me to accept the oneness in life. Perhaps that is the secret of the seventh heaven, the place of extreme joy, which I know I'll be passing through soon. Our talks have given me a comforting vision of that transition. It's my hope that when my body dies, my soul will become one with the Infinite. And then I will finally get to see the Face of God."

First Heaven

Lighting Your Own Candle

Life on Earth

Second Heaven

Gathering the Sparks

The Present is Part of Eternity

Third Heaven

Sheltering the Flame

Protecting Your True Inner Voice

Fourth Heaven

Brightening the Flame

Accepting Being Human

Fifth Heaven

Illuminating the Way

Angels on Earth

Sixth Heaven

Lighting the Next Candle

Passing the Torch

Seventh Heaven

Becoming One with the Light

Seeing the Face of God

A NEW DAY

IT IS SUNDAY morning at 9:30 a.m. I am in my office, going over some papers. At 10:00 a.m., I take the elevator to the seventh floor to visit a patient who has asked to see me. Afterwards I walk down to the fifth floor to find out how Jonathan is doing. I knock on his door but there is no reply. I open the door and see that the room has been cleaned and prepared for the next occupant. The bed is neatly made and everything is in its place. I notice a small white envelope on the table next to the bed. I walk closer and see that it is addressed to me. I open it and find this note inside, in Jonathan's handwriting:

> *Dear Rabbi,*
>
> *Wherever I am on my journey, I am alone and happy in my aloneness. I finally recognize that my aloneness allowed me to be creative throughout my lifetime. By accepting my aloneness, I am also more able to face death.*
>
> *Thank you for getting me that copy of the picture on my wall. It is a wonderful gift. I have taken it with me and I find it comforting. I think it reminds me of the continuity of a beautiful world. I also realize, at last, that the boat at the dock is longing for the open sea.*

Do you remember when you told me about Carlos, about how he wanted to go home to die? I also want to go home to die. But I know that I can find that place, that 'home,' inside me, not in a particular building.
Don't worry about me. I am sailing on the high seas.

I love you and all of life.
Jonathan

I am very moved by Jonathan's words. I walk over to the painting that meant so much to him and gaze at it intently, looking at the painted horizon that is visible over the bow of the ship. I make out some small specks of color that I have never noticed before. They are birds! I see that they are flying out to sea.

I walk over to the windows. The drapes are completely pulled back, allowing light to stream into the room. It is the beginning of a new day.

EPILOGUE

Dear Jonathan and Dear Reader,

Wherever you are on your journey through life, I hope these words have touched your spirit and lifted your heart. The more we understand and learn about the nature of our lives, the more comfortable we will be in thinking about *all* aspects of life, including the dying process.

Death never comes at the "right" time. For some, it seems to arrive much too early; for others, it seems to come too late. We have only one choice: to respond and create a lasting legacy. Death, whenever it comes, can be our final stage of growth.

Let me share with you the story of a remarkable woman who helped me understand how death can be transformed into a meaningful, even uplifting experience for both patient and family.

Emily was in her late thirties and the mother of three. Diagnosed with an inoperable brain tumor, she underwent outpatient treatment, including radiation. But her condition quickly worsened. She was admitted to the hospital and it soon became evident that the end was near. She would never return home.

What made the situation more poignant was that her oldest child, Steven, was due to become Bar Mitzvah the following month. He, along with the rest of the family, realized that his mother could not possibly hold on that long. As Emily was given higher doses of medication and began to sleep for longer and longer periods of time, her family and close friends consulted me about conducting a special ceremony. We decided to hold a Bar Mitzvah service that very afternoon, right in Emily's room. There, surrounded by her entire family, she would be able to share in the celebration of her son's coming of age.

An aunt drove Steven back to his house, where he changed into his Bar Mitzvah suit and picked up a copy of the formal speech he had prepared for the occasion. As soon as he returned, I took the Torah from the ark in the hospital's chapel and carried it to Emily's room. Several people accompanied me, including the compassionate oncologist who had been treating Emily.

I set the Torah down on the tray table next to her bed, welcomed everyone and called Steven up to read his portion from the scroll. He did a fine job, singing each note in a strong, clear, confident voice. His mother beamed with pride. After Steven recited the blessings, we all shouted "Mazel Tov."

Then Steven, Emily's oncologist and I joined hands with the other guests and began to dance, some of us on one side of the bed and some on the other. As each of us danced near the window, the afternoon sunlight illuminated the tears glistening on our cheeks.

After we concluded our dancing and singing, I finally asked Steven if he would like to deliver the speech he had prepared. He nodded, but as he moved towards the head of the bed, he put aside his prepared text and turned to face his mother. He then began to speak from his heart. He thanked his mother for all she had done for him and expressed his eternal love and admiration for her.

Emily could barely speak. But somehow she found the strength to respond. With tears in her eyes, she gazed with admiration at her eldest child. Then she spoke. Her words, like Steven's, conveyed her deep love for him and for her entire family, along with her spirit of hope. When she finished, she and Steven hugged and kissed. The room was filled with complete silence. We all knew we were witnessing a holy moment.

No one spoke for a long time. Then, each member of the family and each friend slowly made their way to the head of the bed, gazed into Emily's eyes and embraced her. She appeared to be very tired, yet very serene. Her husband asked her if she would like to rest and she nodded her agreement. We quietly left the room. Emily died peacefully later that night.

The power of that ceremony continues to touch all of us who were privileged to participate in it.

Almost a year has passed since that celebration. Several weeks ago, Emily's oncologist was paged to respond to an emergency call. When he picked up the phone, he found Steven on the other end of the line.

"Doctor, do you remember me? This is Steven, Emily's son. I'm sorry to catch you at such a busy time, but there's an urgent matter I need to discuss with you. You know, I'm only 14, but I've already decided what I want to be when I grow up. I want to be an oncologist just like you. I want to help people, just like you helped my Mom until the very last minute. You've got to tell me which classes to take and which journals to read in order to prepare for my future."

The physician, who is not only wise, but also understanding, told Steven which classes to sign up for the following semester and which medical journals he could begin to become acquainted with. He promised to be Steven's academic guide all the way through medical school and beyond.

Emily nurtured herself and her family throughout her life. Although her years were tragically few, she lived to see the seeds of

217

her labors bear fruit. Those fruits carry seeds of their own. The cycle continues.

Emily taught us that no matter what life had brought her, no matter how unfair her illness and early passing appeared to be, she had not given up on life. She could still smile. She could still sing. She realized life would go on, that the world would continue and that her children would be part of that future. When she spoke of hope, she spoke from her heart.

Emily's message of optimism, of looking forward even in the face of despair, was transmitted to her son, as well as to every one of us around her bed. She taught us a lesson about *life*, not about death. Her physician, the other care givers and her friends demonstrated how the compassion of those around us can make every second of life feel precious and unforgettable.

I hope that the story of Emily, as well as those of the other unique individuals that I have shared, will help you confront your own journey. I welcome the chance to hear from you and to learn how you are approaching this most significant event of your life. I am genuinely interested in understanding how you have dealt with other major transitions in your life and what brings you the most comfort. I hope that my words, no matter how they may differ from your beliefs, will help us engage in a genuine dialogue of mutual respect and caring.

Thank you for accompanying me on my journey as I talk about the issues that are central to our existence. I can only offer you my love, my heart and my hand. I would like to be there to hold your hand in some way on your final journey. I want to accompany you in a way that will be meaningful for you and for those who love you.

I pray that on your journey through life, you rejoice in the beauty, the goodness and the radiance of yourself and those around you –

your family and your soul friends. By doing so, your life can become a manifestation of energy and light on earth. That can be your most precious legacy, as your flame continues to illuminate the world forever.

I would appreciate hearing from readers who want to share their thoughts and experiences. If you would like to contact me, please write to:

Cedars-Sinai Medical Center
8700 Beverly Blvd.
Los Angeles, California 90048

ABOUT THE AUTHOR

Rabbi Levi Meier, Ph.D., is the Jewish Chaplain at Cedars-Sinai Medical Center in Los Angeles, CA, and he is also a clinical psychologist in private practice. He has experienced Jungian analysis from both sides of the couch. He has listened and related to thousands of patients over the years, from whom he has distilled the commonalities of the human struggle and the multiple paths towards self-fulfillment. Rabbi Meier lives with his wife, Marcie, and family in Los Angeles.